KU-547-362

Democracy and the European Union

Theory, Practice and Reform

Alex Warleigh

SAGE Publications
London • Thousand Oaks • New Delhi

First published 2003

 SAGE Publications Ltd
6 Bonhill Street
London EC2A 4PU

SAGE Publications Inc.
2455 Teller Road
Thousand Oaks, California 91320

SAGE Publications India Pvt Ltd
B-42, Panchsheel Enclave
Post Box 4109
New Delhi 110 017

British Library Cataloguing in Publication data

A catalogue record for this book is available
from the British Library

ISBN 0 7619 7280 3
ISBN 0 7619 7281 1 (pbk)

Library of Congress Control Number 2002112352

Typeset by C&M Digitals (P) Ltd., Chennai, India
Printed in Great Britain by Athenaeum Press, Gateshead

For Christopher, who believes the book will be
dedicated to him, and so it is.

This is also for Mrs P. and She, with thanks for their fabulous
performances in a Supporting Role. No tears now, ladies, just
take the trophy and get off the dais.

Contents

Acknowledgements

Writing a book such as this the author inevitably incurs debts to many people, particularly if, as in the present case, it draws on a decade or so of research into, thinking about, and even 'doing' European integration.

I would like to thank Lucy Robinson at Sage for her kind extension to my deadline and being so positive about the project in general. The Leverhulme Trust (Grant F/239/AA), the European Commission (TSER Contract SOE2-CT97-3056) and the ESRC (Grant L213 25 2022) provided generous funding for different aspects of the research undertaken for this book. My partners in the EURCIT network made many helpful contributions to the evolution of my thinking over several years, and my thanks go to all of them, but to Richard Bellamy, Dimitris Chryssochoou, Dario Castiglione, Andreas Follesdal, and Jo Shaw a special debt is due. Students at Reading and Belfast also made me probe and question some of my thinking, even if they weren't always aware of this! My thanks go in particular to the students who took my MA course at Reading in 'Democracy and Reform in the EU'.

Richard Bellamy, Ciarán O'Kelly and Elizabeth Meehan provided very helpful feedback on drafts of some of the chapters in this book. As usual, I am indebted to them for their insights and remain responsible for any remaining shortcomings in the text.

Finally, I owe thanks to all those friends and family who bore with me as I completed this book not in the hoped-for sabbatical term but as an accompaniment to taking up a new post in Belfast. I look forward to rediscovering what weekends and evenings are for.

Preface: Thoughts of a Critical European

This is *not* a Eurosceptic book. It does not seek to challenge the legitimacy of the European integration project itself, but rather to uncover why some of the various strategies that the EU institutions and member states have used to improve the EU's democratic credentials have not worked successfully. I do not think that these failures were inevitable because the EU itself is in some way irretrievably flawed or powerless. Neither do I think these failures are impossible to rectify. Indeed, the last chapter of this book draws conclusions about how the process of democratisation in the EU could be advanced. To that end, I have tried to be historically literate and to draw on political history, political theory, legal science, international relations, and EU studies literatures, as well as empirical evidence gained through original primary research.

However, this book does challenge some of the conventional wisdom about how the EU might be made more democratic – from both pro- and anti-integration perspectives. I ask the reader to lay aside, or at least question, some of the easy assumptions made by both groups about the European integration process, that I think are in danger of becoming rival, unquestionable catechisms. The mere fact that this book does not argue in favour of a European Federation does not make it an intergovernmentalist tome. In fact, as I make clear throughout the book, I lay no great normative significance on the concept of national sovereignty. In other publications, I have demonstrated both theoretically and empirically that the national governments of the EU – which might be considered its principal contracting parties – do not, and should not, control every meaningful aspect of the integration process or the EU political system. I do, however, attach great importance to the idea of *popular sovereignty*, and it is for that reason that my concern with improving the democratic credentials of the EU has been so enduring.

I am conscious that as someone whose political identity is perceived as British (and, moreover, English), it may seem to those in other member states that my approach to the European integration project is predictably cautious. At least, so it appears to have seemed to many colleagues from other member states, who conveniently forget that for every Margaret Thatcher there is a Charles de Gaulle, Umberto Bossi or Edmund Stoiber, not to mention 'restless natives' in Denmark and the Irish Republic. This *oubli* is even more ironic given that unlike many academics, I actually devoted a year of my life to working in the European Parliament, in order to help, in a small way, improve the content of EU legislation and reinforce the Parliament in its day-to-day encounters with the national governments and other EU institutions.

As an academic, I consider it my duty to be critical in my thinking: evaluative, reflective, and, as far as possible, objective. I do not subscribe to any theoretical or strategic view of European integration without questioning it. As a long-standing member of the European Movement, I believe profoundly that the European Union has much to offer as a model and instrument of political, economic and social organisation which transcends (yes, that word!) the nation state. As a lifelong holder of political principles towards the Left/Ecological end of the traditional spectrum, however, I also cannot help but be aware of ways in which the current EU might be improved. My aim, and hope, for this book is that it will make a positive contribution to the ongoing debate about EU democratic reform, and thereby help ensure that the EU is as central to the European continent's good governance in the 21st century as it was to the post-World War II recovery of its Western half.

Alex Warleigh
Belfast

1

Introductory Overview: The 'Democratic Deficit' and the Normative Turn in European Union Studies

European integration has never been democratic. Instead, the process of constructing the Euro-polity has been about securing conditions in which democracy is a viable proposition. Initially, this meant shoring up a largely national project of reform and rebuilding after the ravages of war, by cementing that process in a calculated condition of economic interdependence which was to lead to eventual political union of a nebulous kind. Currently, this means constructing both different ways of running the idiosyncratic political system that European integration has produced, and facilitating the willingness and capacity of the everyday citizen to engage with the making of policy decisions in that system.

Most observers of the present day European Union (EU, the Union) agree that the EU suffers from a 'democratic deficit' which it must rectify in order to justify its continued existence and expansion. However, there is no agreement about what the EU should do to solve the problem. Moreover, insufficient attention has been paid to the strategies employed by both EU institutions and the member governments of the Union to remedy the situation *qua* strategies of democratic reform rather than as matters of institutional change or indicators of the success/failure/potential of the integration process in general. These reform strategies break down into four main categories: reconfiguring national sovereignty (subsidiarity and flexibility); institutional change (e.g. the gradual empowerment of the European Parliament); change in the scope and powers of the Union (e.g. enhanced capacities in cohesion and social policies, the creation of the second and third 'pillars' of the Union, dedicated respectively to the common foreign and security policy and police and judicial cooperation); and the attempted creation of a European 'demos' by such mechanisms as EU citizenship and quasi-corporatist Union policy-making. The novelty of this book is its exploration of the paradox of European integration, namely that despite successive reforms which make the EU more in keeping with the liberal democratic model of the state – and thus conventional wisdom of what constitutes democracy – the democratic deficit persists at EU level and appears to be worsening at member state level too.

The central hypothesis of this book is that the principal obstacles in the EU's path to democratic reform are deficits of legitimacy[1] and participation. Despite adaptations of the ways in which the Union works, it remains unpopular for three main reasons. First, the Union's competences do not reflect those that the public considers it should have (Blondel et al. 1998). Second, the citizen remains on the periphery of the decision-making process of the EU despite efforts to create both symbolic legitimacy for, and new political opportunity structures in, the Union (Wiener 1998; see also the essays in Bellamy and Warleigh 2001). Third, the EU is the most visible example of what Andersen and Burns (1996) call 'post-parliamentary governance', and thus suffers disproportionately from criticisms based on problems common to all the member states, i.e. the shift towards the dominance of the executive and the expert over the elected representative, and the rise of issue, rather than partisan, politics.

This book explores the various strategies deployed to enhance the Union's democracy since the Single European Act 1986, and assesses their ability to reduce the 'democratic deficit' both singly and collectively. It sets out a new understanding of what the 'democratic deficit' really means – the lacuna that I dub the 'functional–ideational gap', in which system needs and advances produce problems of democracy which cannot be solved through the use of orthodox methods or state-based models of democracy. I argue that in order for this problem to be solved the Union must take radical action. It must match its competences more closely with those deemed legitimate for transnational governance by the public, and increase the ability of citizens to participate in the making of the decisions which increasingly impact upon their lives. Rather than make half-hearted attempts at reform based on liberal democracy, the Union must seek more imaginative solutions appropriate for its transnational nature.

These claims, and an appropriate theoretical framework, are substantiated in Chapter 2. Initially, however, it is necessary to provide an overview of the literature on the democratic deficit. Consequently, the task attempted in Chapter 1 is to ask and answer four key questions:

1 What is the 'democratic deficit', and how did it arise?
2 Why has there been a 'normative turn' in EU studies, and what does it entail?

3 How is democracy best defined in the EU context?
4 What models of democracy beyond the state exist, and how can they
applied to the EU?

What is the 'democratic deficit', and how did it arise?

Defining the democratic deficit

When commentators, politicians and everyday citizens maintain that the
EU's democratic credentials are inadequate, what do they really mean? Is
there one commonly agreed understanding of what democracy means and
how it must be expressed institutionally, which could simply be applied to
the EU and remove the perception of a problem in an instant? Clearly, there
is no such miracle cure, and this should be no surprise. Concepts such as
democracy are open to a variety of interpretations whose importance is not
simply academic (Arblaster 1987). Struggles over what democracy means,
and the degree of individual freedom and responsibility with which it is
compatible, have coloured political life since at least the French Revolution.
Thus, one of the difficulties of defining the democratic deficit is the existence of rival understandings of what democracy is, and how it could best
be applied to the EU (see the section on models of democracy. Further
difficulties are caused by the fact that defining democracy in the EU context
cannot be done without taking into account other contested notions such
as national sovereignty. This is because those seeking to democratise the EU
have to ask and answer a very pointed set of questions. Whose interests
should be pre-eminent in EU decision-making: those of the states, which initiated and continue to hold most power in the process of European integration, or those of the citizens, in whose name the process is supposedly
being carried out? Would it be best to find a way to mix the two? Would it
be possible to find an appropriate balance? If so, what criteria should be
applied to the design of an appropriate system? And would the system, and
the balance which underpins it, be enduring or in need of regular revision
in order to maintain legitimacy? These are the issues of principle and debate
over which academics, federalists and defenders of national independence
argue.

Furthermore, it is necessary to be clear about why democracy matters.
Why does it matter that political systems are aligned with principles of legitimacy, accountability, transparency, participation, and equality more than
with, say, those of efficiency? Being 'democratic' may make a system less
efficient by restricting what those in power can rightfully do and by slowing down decision making so that opportunities are lost. In short, democracy can make a political system less able to produce optimally successful

public policy (Saward 1994). Should we prioritise a democratic process of participation (by which citizens shape the decisions made by public authorities) or a democratic process of accountability (by which citizens are/must be satisfied with holding decision-makers responsible for their public actions, and by which decision-makers seek to produce policies in line with what they perceive to be public opinion)? Of course, the two views are not mutually exclusive, but as is made clear in the essays of Beetham's (1994) collection this does not mean that democratic theorists, and politicians, have not advocated one form rather than another and wrought corresponding social change.

We must remember that there is an obvious gap between ideal-type models of democracy and actual practice of governance in states usually considered 'democratic', such as (to take just a few examples) Spain, the USA, the UK, Italy or Sweden. Theories of democracy tend to promote utopian views of the 'good polity' to which real life will always find it difficult, if not impossible, to correspond. This should not be taken to mean that democracy is a meaningless or hopelessly relativistic concept. It *should* be taken to mean, however, that if we consider democracy to be important, we must be clear about what we want it for, and what challenges to it we are prepared to uphold in the name of the greater good (e.g. should we have an absolute right to free speech, or is it better to place certain restrictions on it to ensure public safety?).

Yet another factor for consideration is the need to distinguish between what Kaldor and Vejvoda (1999: 3–4) call *formal* and *substantive* kinds of democracy. Formal democracy focuses on the design of a legitimate and fair set of procedures, rules and institutions, such as the establishment of the rule of law. Substantive democracy is 'a process that has to be continually reproduced, a way of regulating power relations in such a way as to maximise the opportunities for individuals to influence the conditions in which they live, to participate in and influence debates about the key decisions that affect society' (Kaldor and Vejvoda 1999: 3). Thus, formal democracy, advocated by such theorists as Schumpeter (1976), is not primarily about active participation by citizens, but rather about providing legitimate leadership and mechanisms to choose between rival candidates for public office (as well as to dismiss leaders whose performance is deemed unsatisfactory). Substantive democracy, advocated by theorists such as Held (1988), gives centrality to an active civil society and widespread public participation in political life. In the case of European integration, we need to consider whether formal democracy is sufficient, and if not how best to combine it with, and encourage, a more substantive model.

Schmitter (1998; 2000) is right to argue that because the EU is clearly more than an international organisation, albeit less than a new state, it now requires greater attention to be paid to its democratic credentials in order to safeguard its positive achievements (see below). Perhaps the best help here, however, is a normative rather than a strategic view. Abraham Lincoln's famous call at Gettysburg (1863) for government of the people, by the people, for the people is instructive: it reminds us that collective decisions need to be made in circumstances of fallibility (i.e. things can go wrong), and that the best way to make sure that this happens both fairly and in a way which allows mistakes to be rectified is to ensure that everyone has access to, and a role to play in, the decision-making process. In turn, this process must be directed towards ensuring fair outcomes for all. Lincoln's call also reminds us straight away that democracy is about ensuring popular control of public decision-making: the emphasis is placed on individual action (citizenship) rather than trust in 'experts' or (even benevolent) dictators to run public life for us. These criteria remind us why democracy matters from the point of view of political principle: it enables the relatively powerless a degree of control over the actions of the powerful, and ensures that, to borrow from Orwell, no one is more equal than anyone else. But even so, these criteria leave open a number of questions about the mechanics of democracy, i.e. exactly how popular control should be exerted over decision-making, and the extent to which equality should be pursued (for example, to ensure political equality, do we also need social equality?). These concerns are not academic arcana, but rather values and goals whose pursuit has produced many different outcomes, not to mention conflicts, over time in any given country.

The statement that the EU has a democratic deficit thus requires much elucidation if it is to be credible. It is necessary to take Beetham's (1994) criteria of political control and equality, and spell out exactly what they (should) mean in the context of the EU. It is also necessary – and this is the key step – to investigate why the EU is so much less successful in presenting itself as a democratic entity than its member states, none of which are in reality anything like paragons of democratic virtue as judged against most, if not all, theories of democratic governance (Andersen and Burns 1996: 267). It is also necessary to uncover why the EU is perceived to have a problematic relationship with democracy when, as Harste (1998) argues, its construction is being undertaken in a more open, more participatory and less coercive fashion than was the case for any of its member states. It is also necessary to bear in mind that for most citizens a degree of acceptance of the Union's existence appears to have persisted despite the perception of the democratic deficit. Some commentators have argued that the EU may not be loved, considered to practice 'good governance', or held by individual survey respondents directly to have benefited either themselves or their member states (Eurobarometer 54, Autumn 2000), but to some extent it is accepted by citizens as part of the (necessary) political structure, and therefore in need of reform rather than eradication (Banchoff and Smith 1999;

Cram 2001). If this is true, it is scarcely an endorsement of integration so far; however, it may constitute a foundation upon which democratic reform could build.

Lord (2001) argues that to be credible, a diagnosis of the EU's 'democratic deficit' and advocacy of a remedy must be grounded in an understanding of two further core issues. First, it must weigh up and acknowledge the attempts made so far to democratise the Union (even if these are considered by the observer to have failed). It is vital to recognise that EU politics and policy-making have been reformed in many ways, often explicitly with the goal of creating greater legitimacy, in order to understand the current situation. Second, a successful diagnosis/prescription must provide a means by which normative argument about values, rather than simply structures, can take place and be acknowledged, because merely refashioning institutions will not solve the underlying sense of inappropriateness if there is no place for reasoned argument and justification of (rival) solutions. In addition, it is necessary to acknowledge that the EU is the only instance of regional integration or international organisation 'where there is an attempt to democratise politics above the level of the state' (Laffan 1998: 249), and that when compared to either organisations like NATO or multinational corporations (i.e. other powerful players in international politics), the EU's democratic record is impressive (Dahl 1989: 320; Laffan et al. 2000).

Features of the democratic deficit

The conventional wisdom about the democratic deficit, however, is that it expresses the lack of fit between the Union and the standard criteria of liberal democracy (see Chapter 2 for a detailed exposition and discussion). Helpfully summed up by Chryssochoou (1998, 2000) as a mixture of institutional and socio-psychological factors, the democratic deficit is a term which refers to the EU's non-standard practices and institutions of decision making, and its inability to generate either a significant shift in loyalties towards itself or a deep sense of shared interests and commonalities between the peoples of the member states. In both formal and substantive terms, the EU can match Beetham's requirements of legitimacy only in small part.

Given that formal democracy is less demanding than the substantive variant, it is sensible to examine the Union's ability to satisfy this form of democracy first. Initial indications here are positive. The member states of the Union enjoy collective control over its ultimate rule-making process, Treaty change, as well as the greatest influence in day-to-day decision-making (Moravcsik 1999). There is thus a sense in which there ought to be no question that the EU is a democratically acceptable organisation, in that power is ultimately wielded by democratically elected national governments. However, this view is only partially correct. The EU is not solely, or even mostly, a tool by which national governments achieve their preferred policy outcomes without significant cost or compromise (Forsyth 1981). By playing the EU game, national governments sacrifice some of their independence in order to secure their objectives, at both macro (system-building) and micro (policy-making) levels; this concession is considered acceptable precisely because states thereby achieve most of their policy objectives. The effective use of state power requires transnational action by governments, and the making of agreements which cannot routinely then be unmade by national institutions such as parliaments. Thus, some form of democracy at the EU level is necessary to make good the loss of democratic control at the national level, even if this does not mean that democracy/democratic control of decision-making is only viable at the new 'European' level (Beetham and Lord 1998; Höreth 1999).

Moreover, actors other than member governments can be highly influential over decision-making (Peterson 1994; Warleigh 2000b), meaning that seeking to rest the EU's legitimacy on that of its member governments cannot be an exclusive strategy. In addition, since the use of qualified majority voting was sanctioned by the Single European Act, no EU citizen can rely upon her or his government to secure the outcomes they have promised, since the unilateral power to block unwanted decisions has been reduced and, in some cases, removed. Furthermore, as Lodge (1994) points out, member governments have been less than quick to reform the democratic credentials of their own institution (the Council), and eager to use the other institutions – especially the Commission – as a scapegoat for the problems in EU democracy/legitimacy. Thus, it is clear that power in the EU is exercised supranationally, that is at a level beyond the member states, albeit in the final analysis by the member states as a collective. Moreoever, although the dominant culture in the Council (and also in its preparatory committees such as COREPER) is one of consensus (Gabel 1998a; Lewis 2000; Sherrington 2000), the practice of deliberation or even bargaining to produce policy outcomes has not yet gone beyond this elite level (Eriksen 2000).

It is also necessary to consider here the fact that the Union has no single decision-making authority which can ultimately be held accountable for EU decisions. In the EU decision-making system, there is no clear separation of powers, either horizontally (that is, between the EU institutions), or vertically (between the EU on the one hand, and its component states and regions on the other). Instead, powers are 'fused' (Wessels 1997) between the national and European tiers to the extent that it can be difficult to identify in practical terms where one ends and the other starts. Moreover, functions of governance are blurred, since they are shared between the institutions and often rely on the informal use of power (Warleigh 2001b). Given that legislative powers are shared between the Council of Ministers, the Commission and the European Parliament (EP), there is no 'government' to be identified and held accountable, nor any opposition able to constitute a rival government to which electors could turn (Neunreither 1998). Insofar as the Commission can be identified as constituting the EU's executive authority, it can reasonably be argued that the EP has increasing powers of scrutiny, as demonstrated by the spectacular resignation of the Commission in 1999 to ward off a vote of no confidence by the EP. However, the EP does not have the ability to appoint a new Commission (which remains a power of the Council), even though Treaty revisions and informal practice have given the EP greater de facto influence in this regard (see Chapter 4).

Setting the EU's legislative agenda is not a function of an elected assembly, but (at least formally speaking) almost entirely the responsibility of the Commission in the first pillar, and national governments in the other two. Decision-making requires the formation of 'policy coalitions' (Warleigh 2000b), issue-specific alliances of actors who pursue mutually beneficial objectives by networking, rather than the party political or issue-based generation of majorities in an assembly (the need to secure a majority in the EP plenary constituting just one of the necessary steps to be taken by those seeking to influence EU policy outcomes). It can, therefore, be very difficult for those outside this process to pinpoint either which actors contributed to each decision or what that contribution actually was. The transparency of the system, then, is low, which obviously makes accountability more difficult.

The rule of law in the EU, or at least in its first pillar, the European Community (EC),[2] is, however, guaranteed. The Treaties on which the EU is based constitute a set of binding rules which member states oblige themselves to observe by their agreement to EU membership and Treaty reform. In short, the rule of law is guaranteed as a means by which member states of the EU can be sure that their partner states can be relied upon to honour their responsibilities, and therefore feel able to limit their own autonomy (Forsyth 1981). The EU has a complex judicature, comprising the European Court of Justice (ECJ) and the Court of First Instance, whose function is to ensure member states accept the rule of law in the EU context, and whose powers to do so are extensive (Hunt 2001). However, the powers of the two EU courts to police the system have not gone unchallenged by either individual citizens or national courts. This is for two important reasons. First, the conflict between national courts and the ECJ over which institution has the right to decide the extent of the EU's powers and the scope of EC law: the 'kompetenz-kompetenz' issue (Hunt 2001). Second, the fact that the Courts' judgments – whether intentionally or not – have been highly influential in guiding the path of European integration, both in terms of shaping or facilitating major policies and in terms of establishing key principles of EU governance (Shaw 1996). For example, the Court's ruling in the *Cassis-de-Dijon* case enabled the Commission to facilitate the single market programme by obviating the need for harmonisation of legislation if an agreed set of common minimum standards could instead be agreed (Alter and Meunier-Aitsahalia 1994). Furthermore, important principles in European integration, such as the supremacy of EU law, direct effect (which gives member state nationals rights that can be invoked directly under national law without the need for an enabling measure by the member state), and member state liability for non-compliance with EU policy, have all resulted from ECJ rulings rather than Treaty change.

Thus, while member states accept the need for the rule of law at EU/EC level, neither they nor EU citizens have wanted the powers of the EU-level institutions set up to guarantee this oversight function themselves to be unchecked. There is debate about whether the member states occasionally seek to check the powers of the Courts as a signal that judicial activism will not be tolerated (Taylor 1975; Weiler 1991), and the extent to which the ECJ is willing and able to influence the EU's policy-making processes (Wincott 1995a, 1995b). Most notably in the case of the Brunner challenge to the Maastricht Treaty, where the German Supreme Court ruled that it, rather than the ECJ, enjoys the ultimate power of 'kompetenz-kompetenz' as far as Germany is concerned, but also in similar cases before other national courts, the assumed supremacy of EC law has not gone unchallenged or unmodified. Genuine concerns about legitimacy can be observed here: given the limits of the scope of EC law, and its predominantly market-making rationale,[3] there must normatively be limits to the ECJ's ability to 'squeeze' flanking measures out of the *acquis communautaire* (the body of EC law and policy) which decision makers have not expressly authorised (Bańkowski and Scott 1996), even if the limits of the Treaty basis themselves act as a more mundane constraint on the ECJ's capacity to add to the acquis (Downes 2001). Thus, for the EU legal system to function effectively, and be normatively acceptable, an ongoing and complex balancing act between national and EU legal orders is necessary (Joerges 1996). While the principle of the rule of law is easy to accept, the precise means by which it can be ensured is more difficult to specify.

Even in terms of formal democracy, the EU system can be deemed inadequate, chiefly as a result of its compromised transparency. It has an effective system of decision-making, and has generated much useful public policy. Nonetheless, the EU's unclear separation of powers and complex, network-based method of decision-making render the system excessively opaque and thereby hinder accountability. The construction of a suitable EC/EU legal order to ensure the rule of law is another complex and ongoing process, and appears to be guaranteed through a process of dialogue between the EU and national courts rather than by the establishment of a clearly hierarchical (and thus transparent) system (Shaw 1996).[4] In substantive terms, however, the balance sheet is even more in debit, given the immense participation deficit which is in turn composed of shortfalls in both the practice of citizenship and the expression of a Europeanised political identity.

To be 'substantively democratic', as indicated above by Kaldor and Vejvoda (1999), a political system must provide regular opportunities for citizens to engage with the decision-making process, and citizens must routinely take up such opportunities. Thus, institutional and affective factors must be sufficient; system structure and individual agency must reinforce each other. Given the shortcomings in the Union's institutional structure, it is unsurprising that opportunity structures for, and their use by, EU citizens are inadequate – that is, there are insufficient, and insufficiently effective, opportunities for the citizen to engage with the process of EU decision-making. These shortcomings make a participation deficit inevitable, but it is worth briefly examining here the concepts of EU citizenship and 'European' identity to illustrate the point.[5] This is especially so given that contemporary views of what democracy is tend to privilege the idea of solidarity between and engagement by citizens rather than action in the perceived public interest by paternalistic elites (March and Olsen 1995: 5–6).

A limited form of EU citizenship was formally established by the Maastricht Treaty as a result of synergies created between certain member states' concerns about the democratic deficit and the concerns of others about enabling sufficient freedom of movement for the successful operation of the single market (Warleigh 2001c: 21–3). EU citizenship is a complement to, and not a replacement for, national citizenships, but also a means by which member state nationals are given a formal link with both nationals of other member states and the EU institutions. Thus, it is an entirely novel status (Meehan 1993), and one which is in principle capable of transforming the way in which the EU and those it governs relate to each other. However, its development to date has been limited (Magnette 1999); formally speaking, Maastricht has so far marked the high point of EU citizenship, as Treaty reforms at both Amsterdam and Nice failed to reduce the tensions between its economic and political rationales or add to the rights, privileges and duties (the latter being currently non-existent) that it confers. In terms of informal citizenship, it has been argued that citizens are increasingly mobilising at EU level, and certainly non-governmental organisations other than those representing the private sector, and which can thus be argued to have some status as representatives of certain members of the public (such as Greenpeace or the Worldwide Fund for Nature), have been able to acquire greater influence over EU decision-making (Greenwood 1997; Warleigh 2000b). However, it remains to be seen whether such actors really do possess effective links to the public, and whether members of the public are really enabled to engage with EU decision-making by membership of or support for such groups (Warleigh 2001a).

The creation of a European identity has proved similarly difficult. As Shore and Black (1994) point out, this is unsurprising since the generation of European identity in the member states of the Union relies upon the public adoption of a different rationale for the European integration project than that which is normally espoused by national politicians (economic benefits, rather than the development and defence of shared interests). Currently, Europeans (here, member state nationals) tend to emphasise their diversity rather than what they have in common, and have failed to be persuaded otherwise by the adoption of EU symbols of common identity such as the flag, hymn and passport. In addition, there is no coherent 'other' against whom Europeans could define themselves collectively. With the end of the Cold War there is no threatening Soviet Union to act as the repository of all things which somehow aren't 'us'. The divide between East and West in Europe is now also far less evident, being socio-economic, or perhaps cultural, rather than military/political; when talking of a 'European' identity it is no longer possible to restrain its scope to EU member states in any analytically sound way. This is welcome in terms of inclusion; but in terms of defining what is 'European' it means we must reject views based on the Western half of the continent and start a more complex task of integrating Eastern and Western traditions. Moreover, given the extent of ethnic intermingling and migration on the continent, it has always been difficult to define where 'Europe' begins and ends, not just geographically but also culturally and ethnically, a situation which remains unchanged (Davies 1997).

In addition, and partly as a result, collective notions of 'Europe' tend to flow into notions of 'the West' very easily at both elite and popular levels. An example can be taken from contemporary global politics. Perhaps the most edifying aspect of the 'war on terrorism' pursued by the USA at the time of writing is the care taken by many politicians in the USA and Europe not to demonise muslims as an 'other' against which the West could be defined. Even had this step been taken, however, given the need to create an international justificatory coalition, the two categories would have been 'the West' vs 'Islam', not 'Europe' vs 'Islam'. Moreover, at the individual level, those people predisposed to mould their sense of political identity so far as to be 'activists beyond borders' (to use the term of Keck and Sikkink, 1998) tend to be global, rather than parochially European, or American, in their intentions (Klein 2000).

However, as Howe (1995) points out, diversity is not necessarily a barrier to the Europeanisation[6] of identity. Indeed, if we do not have 'unity in diversity' (to use one of the Commission's slogans) it is unlikely that we will have unity at all – not only would there be insurmountable resistance to the development of a homogenised identity, there would be no political will or capacity to create one. In Howe's view what is necessary for the Europeanisation of identity is the acknowledgement of difference between both individuals and groups, accompanied by a long-term process of social communication. Modern societies generate a sense of identity which owes more to shared values and beliefs than shared group experience, given the advent of increased pluralism, multiculturalism and individualism. Difference may matter less than the belief that individuals have some kind of mutual connection. Over time, structure (the EU) will shape identity by its very existence and iterated use. This could be reinforced by a deliberate process of reinvention of national histories and identities in the light of common experience, because such identities were themselves constructed and are not necessarily unchanged (Howe 1995: 28–34).

While usefully critical of both rigid definitions of identity and the alleged importance of ethnic similarity in identity formation, this view is not entirely successful. First, it ignores the EU's weakness in formal democracy: it is difficult for citizens to engage with the Union in the way Howe would like, and thus the experiences of EU level political activity they have may well be negative rather than likely to produce a positive identification with the process. Second, it underplays the difficulty of devising the means to 'glue together' the citizens of different member states in a new community of values.

Howe is right that belief systems shape how we view the world, and thus that the *belief* that individuals have much in common can be more important than whether or not they actually do. He is also right that the perception of likely material benefits from collaboration, and the absence of any single (national) identity in the new European space which is powerful enough to cause citizens with other identities to fear 'swamping' by it, both facilitate the generation of a Europeanised identity for EU citizens (Gabel 1998b). However, it is necessary to be cautious about the extent of public perception of material gains from integration – according to Eurobarometer 54 (Autumn 2000), only 47% of member state nationals consider that their country has benefited from its membership of the EU. Moreover, Howe's view of how that belief can be created is excessively reliant on a powerful central agency which, in the case of the EU, is simply not present given its complex power and institutional structures. In addition there are real ethical considerations here: it is conceivable that at some point in the future a suitably charismatic and powerful EU leadership could arise and successfully carry out a process of identity-generation by social engineering. But would such a 'European' process be any more acceptable from a normative point of view than it was at national level? Would it avoid or replicate the creation of false or half-true myths? Would it avoid or seize the opportunity to use identity generation as an unjust means of exclusion? There can be no a priori confidence that such temptations would be avoided, and a sense of identity artificially erected in an ultimately self-defeating, system de-legitimising manner (as in the attempt to create 'new Soviet man').

Laffan (1996) has argued that a European identity can be shaped successfully only if it is of a civic nature (i.e. centred on values enshrined at the core of the political system and envisaged as a means by which individuals elect to collaborate despite their difference as a result of these shared values). There is no place for myths of a common past in this model, nor for any attempt to construct an identity based on a supposedly common European cultural heritage (which is in fact common only at a very broad level, and is in many ways difficult to distinguish from 'Western' values/practices in general). Thus, despite the fact that the depth of European integration means that traditional views of national identity are redundant in the member states, it is necessary to construct a different, shared sense of identity with great care in order to avoid backlash. The prospective enlargement of the EU to the countries of Central and Eastern Europe, plus the micro-states of Cyprus and Malta and, eventually, Turkey can only underline the futility of attempts to posit or construct any other kind of European(ised) identity, given the great differences in political culture between the states set to join the Union and those which are already members – themselves a highly diverse group.

For this reason, authors such as Chryssochoou (2001a) argue that the major problem of democracy in the EU is the question of how to encourage EU citizens to participate actively in the integration process, constructing in the process a politically-defined 'demos' based on a civic identity. This is because only by such engagement – or 'citizenship practice', to use Wiener's (1998) term – is it likely that citizens will be able either to shape what the EU policy process produces, or generate, via the creation of transnational alliances with other citizens, any real sense of shared interests to be pursued together via the structures of the EU. Of course, this view assumes a link between stakeholding and transfer of at least some loyalty to the EU, and it is true that citizens might simply reproduce the behaviour of interest groups, which tend to use the EU instrumentally rather than out of pro-European zeal (Greenwood and Ronit 1994; Reising 1998). However, it is also true that without providing the means for currently alienated citizens to be socialised into the EU system, it is unlikely that they will accord the Union greater legitimacy than is the case now or identify with it more profoundly than indicated at present.

Origins of the democratic deficit

It must be remembered that the primary goal of those who set up what is now the EU was to preserve the peace in (Western) Europe, thereby establishing a framework in which war-torn economies could be revived and security guaranteed. The tools by which this was to be done were American military and financial support, the deliberate re-establishment of the idea of the state and the state's transformation into a supplier of public welfare such as health and education services (Milward 1994). A process of interlinking these newly established/reformed states economically, in an effort to produce eventual political union of some kind, was a further strand of this strategy. All this was considered a matter of high politics and inter-state diplomacy, not requiring popular consent and participation. Indeed, such input would in all likelihood prevent the process reaching maturity, given the depth of post-war tensions and lack of understanding of international politics of the majority (Monnet 1978). When it had reached the appropriate depth and scope of interlinkage, the process could be democratised. But until that point had been reached, it was paramount to preserve that process, in the hope that its provision of ever greater public welfare would justify both the strategy and the objectives of integration to the citizens, who would eventually waken to its importance (Bellamy and Warleigh 1998).

It goes without saying that European integration was, and is, a worthy goal. In the Europe of the late-1940s, economic prosperity and peace could not be taken for granted. Neither could it simply be assumed that viable, democratically legitimate structures of governance could be erected. As Hobsbawm (1994, Chapter 5) demonstrates, 19th century assumptions about the triumph of liberal democracy hung in tatters even before the events of 1939–45. Totalitarian regimes had been, in many cases, Europe's response to economic decline and the already-evident lessening role of the individual European powers as actors on the world stage. Bourgeois (or liberal) values of constitutional, limited government had often been swept aside as the necessary conditions for their survival (widespread consent; relative cohesion of the 'demos', or people, bound together in a state; limited functions of government; creation of greater prosperity) were erased. Extreme forms of nationalism questioned the viability of many existing state structures and borders; the inter-war Wilsonian project of finding a state for every nation (and thereby removing irredentism as a cause of war) failed in its mission, as the ethnic jigsaw of Europe made it impossible to avoid creating many states in which people of different ethnic origin were both thrown together and provided with an external focus for their loyalties. Moreover, states which had been newly created, or whose borders had been redrawn, could regularly make the case that they should have been constituted otherwise, or that their 'natural' citizenries had been artificially rent asunder. Thus, potential for ethnic strife – or its use a legitimising excuse for war – was not removed, summed up most terribly in the Nazi quest for *Lebensraum* and a unified German *Volk*. European countries such as Germany, Italy, Russia (the former Soviet Union) and Spain developed regimes which were explicitly opposed to liberal democratic values and practices, often through bitter and bloody civil wars, over a period of roughly 20 years from 1917 (Soviet Union) to 1939 (Spain).

The tasks of government in Europe increased enormously as a response to the Great Depression. As argued by Hobsbawm (1994), this was a blow for pre-war democracies in two ways: both conceptually and practically. First, conceptually, reform of the liberal state ate at the heart of the values upon which it had been based (limited government, with a strong role for civil society, now endangered by increasing bureaucratisation and a seemingly ever-greater role for the state in public life). While the reworking of liberal principles was hardly impossible, this process conceded, rightly, that some of the arguments raised against them were not without justification. Liberal democracy was in fact under attack from both right and left of the political spectrum. The Russian Revolution of 1917 set up the world's first Communist regime, and Marxist-Leninist ideologies were both popular and feared in other European countries. Socialist and communist parties were formed across Europe, acting as a focal point for the many who were dispossessed and disenfranchised by the prevailing regimes. Parties of the extreme right grew in response to a perceived communist threat, often seeking to defend 'traditional' values against erosion and European societies were riven with ideological conflict. Second, on a practical level, reform of the state created a new range of welfare tasks which governments had to perform in order to secure, or retain, the loyalty of their citizens. Many governments (such as those of Weimar Germany) were simply unable to live up to their new responsibilities, appearing weak and ineffectual.

When the restoration of viable governance structures to Europe was attempted in the aftermath of the Second World War, those in a position to design the new structures had to ensure not just a new form of ideological and conceptual coherence, but political stability and efficiency in a climate in which ideological extremes were still present. In a continent whose political power, economic strength, military might, prestige, cultural preeminence and moral standing had all evaporated in the 31 years between 1914 and 1945 (Davies 1997: 899), this was no small requirement. Fascism had been defeated, but communism had not, and the then incipient Cold War caused many to fear that communism would spread to the Western half of Europe, either through its ideological strength or more crudely through invasion by the Soviet Union (Laqueur 1982: 117–29).

In sum, pre-war changes to liberal democratic practice paled into insignificance beside the sheer scale of the challenge of rebuilding not only

(Western) Europe's economy, but also restoring the belief of Europeans in the possibility that public life could and should be organised efficiently, effectively and justly. Certain European elites had shown themselves clearly capable of the most heinous disrespect of the norms of democratic behaviour: Hitler, Mussolini, Franco and Lenin had not been teleported to Europe from a distant planet of dictators and retained in power by omnipotent aliens, but had rather had their arrival in power made easier by the support of key parts of the national elites, or, in the case of Lenin, German *raison d'état*. However, support for these dictators had also been present at mass level, exemplified by Hitler's arrival in power through a legitimate election and the popularity of both Hitler and Mussolini in many European countries as bulwarks against communism. Thus, there were sound reasons to question whether democracy in Europe was possible, given that the presence of its necessary underpinnings (later described by Almond and Verba, 1963, as the 'civic culture', i.e. an understanding of what it is to live by democratic norms, and the will and capacity to put that understanding into practice) was open to question.

The founders of the EU therefore prioritised elite-centred welfare generation over popular participation – technocracy over democracy. They set in train a process of integration whose very success (in terms of its chequered but definite growth) has led to its biggest crisis. Social engineering by the EU (activism by its institutions in order to promote and deepen the integration process) was considered a legitimate part of the integration process (Monnet 1978) as well as a key means by which it would advance (Haas 1964, 1968). Instead, the EU's institutions face almost constant criticism; the EU is not usually praised for being a system which allows member governments to 'kick upstairs' problems which are domestically intractable, but rather censured as a means by which lowest common denominator (or otherwise unsatisfactory) solutions to these problems are agreed (Gustavsson 1998; Scharpf 1999) or 'external' forces impose unwanted courses of action. As theorists of democracy have argued (Thompson 1997), democratisation does not always follow 'social differentiation' (urbanisation, modernisation, the communications revolution, and the generation of higher living standards): the EU's provision of greater public welfare has not brought it legitimacy, and the 'ethics of integration' (Bellamy and Warleigh 1998) have allowed the European democratic deficit to change form rather than disappear.

The 'normative turn' in EU studies

Unsurprisingly, then, scholars of European integration have begun to pay attention to issues of democracy, provoking a 'normative turn' (Bellamy and Castiglione 2000b) in EU studies. It is not the case that such concerns were wholly absent from EU studies before recent years. For example, scholar-practitioners such as David Mitrany and Altiero Spinelli wrote passionate, and very different, critiques of the early integration process, agreeing on a diagnosis of its deficiencies in legitimacy but disagreeing almost entirely on the best means to rectify them (see Chapter 2). However, it is true that democracy was never a central concern of mainstream integration theorists. Instead, they studied what they considered the mechanics of system-building (neofunctionalism), or the diplomatic processes by which national governments cooperated (intergovernmentalism), according to the dictates of the respective theoretical paradigms. To simplify, neo-functionalists considered that integration was in the public interest, and therefore considerations of democracy could be subsumed in studies of how the system worked and in designing strategies for its reinforcement. Inter-governmentalists considered that democracy was a non-issue for European integration, since the latter was properly understood not as a process of polity-building but as an exercise in member state diplomacy/foreign policy. Consequently, European integration was properly subject to no more, and no less, scrutiny/accountability than any other act of member state foreign policy.

Democracy and legitimacy, then, occupy a higher place on the EU studies agenda – as on the institutional equivalent – than ever before. Before examining recent work on democracy in the EU, however, it is worth explaining in further detail why the normative turn has come about at this particular juncture in EU studies. I argue that there are three related causes. First, the need to respond to official recognition of public perceptions of a democratic deficit, as integration became far more controversial after the Maastricht Treaty (Treaty on European Union, TEU). Second, theoretical trends within the field of integration theory, which has been undergoing a reflexive period after the collapse of orthodox approaches. And third, the increased interest in the EU of scholars from comparative politics, legal science and political philosophy, alerted by the Maastricht Treaty to the fact that the EU embodies a novel kind of polity-in-the-making, where issues of democratisation are likely to be both controversial and challenging.

Reacting to Maastricht

I turn first to the Maastricht Treaty, which contributed to the perception of insufficient democracy in a number of ways. By raising the prospect of a federal outcome to the integration process, it concerned many. By not going far enough towards federalism, it concerned others. And by deepening and rendering more complex the integration process without making its governance practices more participatory, it did little to entice or facilitate greater public socialisation into the project of European unification.

Thanks to the reaction of many citizens, the TEU had a far more difficult birth than its signatories imagined. Indeed, it was almost stillborn: rejected in the first Danish referendum, it passed in France by the narrowest of margins. Referenda are almost always more complex than the 'yes/no' answer to a single question would indicate. For example, the reasons why those in France voted against the Treaty were complex and in many respects not really centred on matters of the EU (Dinan 1999: 151). Nonetheless, it was clear that public disquiet about deepening European integration had grown. In the 1970s public interest in European integration had been relatively low, with exceptional cases such as heightened interest around the time of enlargement to the UK, Ireland and Denmark (1973). This lack of interest was construed by policy-makers at both national and EU levels as quiescence in the integration process, in keeping with the thinking of the founders of the Union that its supposedly obvious-to-all benefits would be enough to guarantee public support for its continuation and deepening. They were confirmed in this view by the fact that after institutional rejection of the Single European Act (SEA) in Denmark (by the Danish parliament, which considered the Act to demand too great a sacrifice of independence), and Ireland (by the Supreme Court, which ruled the Act was incompatible with the Irish constitution), citizens in both cases supported the Act in referenda.

In retrospect, however, it seems clear that popular support for European integration could not have been guaranteed. In the mid-1980s publicity campaigns had to be undertaken not just to exhort member state nationals to take advantage of the new single market, brought about by the SEA, but almost to remind them that the EU existed. The relative stagnation of the integration process in the 1970s, while often overstated, did manage to hide the increasing salience and scope of the Union from the public eye. As Moravcsik puts it, '(t)he SEA returned European integration to public prominence' (1999: 315). However, by the same token, it also signalled the fact that the EU could no longer be written off as inconsequential, and was an entity whose evolution merited closer scrutiny. Given the concerns raised by the Folketing (Danish Parliament) and the Irish Supreme Court, such scrutiny was almost guaranteed. The TEU, then, arose in a climate of increased attention to the integration process at popular level and in the media. Thus, at the very point at which significant steps were taken to aid the Union's democratisation process (at least according to a vaguely federalist blueprint), and at which the EU became a more significant tool for the resolution of real policy problems, public dissatisfaction with the integration process reached a new high.

The principal reason for this seeming paradox is, as stated above, the miscalculated trajectory for the integration project that was adopted by its founders and essentially maintained until the recognition of flexibility as a valid mode of integration in the 1990s (Warleigh 2002a, 2002b). By playing down the nature of integration's ultimate goal (an undefined but definitely political union, usually taken to mean some kind of federation) and emphasising contingencies, instrumentalism, and 'national interest', member governments failed to create (or even seek) a supportive ideology or set of pro-integration values at popular level (Bellamy and Warleigh 1998: 453–6). So, when public support for a step-change in the integration process (the TEU) was sought, it was not forthcoming: permissive consensus, insofar as it existed, did not equate to or necessarily foster active support for a deeper integration process.

The TEU did not create a federal United States of Europe. However, by setting out a detailed plan and schedule for the long-standing goal of economic and monetary union, it was ambitious. It also brought political union much closer by establishing, *inter alia*, EU citizenship, a fledgling common foreign and security policy (which explicitly left as an open possibility that in time the EU could have a common defence system), a nascent bicameral legislature (via the co-decision process, which linked the Council and Parliament in a new relationship, see Chapter 4), deeper cooperation in matters of justice and home affairs, and the principle of subsidiarity. Admittedly, the latter is inherently ambiguous (see Chapter 3), but it was seen by many on both the pro-integration and anti-EU sides of the debate to encompass the federal principle of a vertical separation of powers. Thus, the TEU did deepen the process of integration considerably, and went some way towards replying to federalist arguments that the EU would never have public support if it did not take on a broader range of competences and increase the powers of the European Parliament (Pinder 1991).

However, the Maastricht Treaty also embodied an important peculiarity, explicable as the result of accommodation of different member state interests (Moravcsik 1999) but scarcely laudable as a strategy for promoting European unification: its inability to satisfy either federalists or defenders of national sovereignty, while also failing to generate public engagement with integration as a useful work-in-progress to be partly shaped by popular input. Federalists such as Duff et al. (1994) considered the Treaty flawed in many ways, for example its division of the EU into three pillars. Anti-integrationists were not persuaded that subsidiarity could be used to defend national sovereignty, and considered that integration had in future to be opposed doggedly if national identity and power were to be safeguarded (Spicer 1992). Those seeking to practice their rights as EU citizens have begun a process which may yet lead to a reconfiguration of what it means to be a citizen (Wiener 1998, see also Chapter 6). However, to date both the use made of citizenship rights, and the ability to bring them to bear on the integration process, remain limited (see the essays in Bellamy and

Warleigh 2001). Moreover, little has been done either to simplify the EU's decision-making processes or explain and justify their complexity. Thus, the EU appears overly Byzantine, and is easy to represent as excessively hermetic: scarcely a recipe for encouraging greater public participation.

Consequently, throughout the last ten years there have been real deficits of both advocacy for, and public participation in, European integration. Indeed, reforms made by the Amsterdam Treaty (1997) and Nice Treaty (2000) have been managerial rather than radical as the member states have prioritised the safe launch of the euro over dealing with either the substantive issues posed by the prospective enlargement to the countries of the former Soviet bloc, Malta, Cyprus and (eventually) Turkey or those of democracy (Duff 1997; Neunreither 2000b; Warleigh 2002b). EU decision makers (both national governments and actors in the EU institutions) have acknowledged that the EU has a significant democracy problem, but have been both unable to summon the collective will to search for a solution, and uncertain about the correct strategy, or mix of strategies, to adopt. Thus, part of the reason for the normative turn is the need to acknowledge the depth and complexity of the democratic deficit, and find imaginative ways to remove, or at least lessen, it: a positive case of scholarship following the real-world agenda.[7]

Re-thinking integration theory

The second reason for the normative turn is of an entirely different character: its roots lie in entirely academic debates about the nature and purpose of European integration theory. Democracy and legitimacy within the Europolity are increasingly central subjects of enquiry within this scholarship (Chryssochoou 2000) and part of a conscious reassessment about what the objectives of EU theory should be (Rosamond 2000a, 2000b; Chryssochoou 2001b). Integration theory has undergone radical reform in the recent years, and attention has been moved away from the traditional dialectical debate between neofunctionalism and neorealism. This has created an intellectual space in which normative issues sit well, because the shift in focus has been accompanied by a reflexive mood about the scope and purpose of integration theory.[8]

The reasons for this shift lie in the failures of the traditional approaches to explain or predict the processes of European integration or EU decision making with adequate sophistication.[9] Neofunctionalism began to unravel in the 1960s, when what it had assumed to be a central logic of integration – the 'spillover' process, whereby integration deepened inexorably – was falsified by the intransigence of the then French President, General de Gaulle. De Gaulle resisted an increase in the supranational elements of EU decision-making, and also blocked further enlargement, indicating that neither in terms of power transfer nor in geographical scope did the EU have an uncontested developmental path ahead of it. Although neofunctionalism was capable of revision (see the excellent collection of essays in Lindberg and Scheingold (1971) it never again enjoyed the ascendancy and was even abandoned by its chief exponent, Ernst Haas (1975). Intergovernmentalism filled the resultant gap, considering the EU to be a limited enterprise akin to any other international organisation and dominated by member state defence-through-best-use of national sovereignty. This matched the condition of the integration process in the 1970s fairly well. However, it did not give scholars the ability to understand the impact of EC law on the integration process or appreciate the extent of the changes made to the EU system by the SEA. The latter's 're-launch' of the integration process caught integration theorists by surprise, and caused a renewal of interest in neofunctionalism.

Significantly, however, it was generally recognised that neither traditional approach was sufficiently accurate,[10] and instead it would be necessary to find a theory which could explain and elucidate the integration process's situation at a kind of mid-point on the continuum of outcomes expected by neofunctionalism (a new federal United States of Europe) and intergovernmentalism (an international organisation with no significantly greater powers, autonomy or scope than any other). Scholars focused their attention on an attempt to synthesise the insights of both theories, and thereby produce a combined super-theory (Keohane and Hoffmann 1991; Tranholm-Mikkelsen 1991). This quest proved fruitless, however, because it was impossible to bridge the huge gap between the core assumptions of the two theories and thus generate a new set of norms which could guide the creation of a new paradigm (Warleigh 1998: 6–9). Theorists' attention shifted again. Instead of attempting to generate 'grand narratives' of European integration, they sought to use empirical investigations to understand different aspects of the integration process, in the hope that over time the theoretical insights could be combined in order to make a coherent whole. As signalled by certain observers (Peterson 1994; Warleigh 2000a), this new quest must take place within a specific and coherent framework if it is to be relied upon to generate useful theory. However, the new pluralism in integration theory which O'Neill (2000) has called the 'post-foundational discourse' in the sub-discipline, also reflects a kind of 'back to basics' approach which is elevated to the realm of social science theory by Rosamond (2000a, 2000b).

Rosamond's approach is to insist on appreciation by theorists of two key issues. First, the need to adopt a 'sociology of knowledge' approach to theory, which seeks not only to understand what different schools of thought maintain, but the reasons why their arguments were shaped in a

particular way (bearing in mind such factors as contemporary views of
what theorising in social science involves, as well as why scholars in any
school perceive gaps in pre-existing knowledge and seek to adopt particular
tools and approaches to fill them). Second, the need to be meta-theoretically
literate. This is not because theory construction is necessarily abstruse, but
because it is important to focus on philosophical issues of the purpose and
limits of social scientific theory in order to develop a set of criteria which
can reorient theory-building productively. For Rosamond (2000b: 157) this
means being critically aware of earlier work, able to engage with real-world
issues, and able to avoid false boundaries between areas of political/social
science. In other words, the 'normative turn' applies to the norms of theory
building as well as normative matters raised by integration itself.

Interdisciplinarity and normative issues

The third contributing factor to the normative turn is the attention paid to
the EU by scholars from different branches of political/social science, and
indeed different disciplines altogether, in keeping with Rosamond's plea
for interdisciplinarity. Much useful and insightful work has been undertaken not just by scholars of comparative politics (e.g. Hix 1999) and
'Europeanists', but also by legal scholars and political theorists. These
scholars have been intrigued by the advent of a novel kind of Euro-polity
and seek above all to elaborate the means by which the EU can achieve a
legitimate and workable new constitutional and normative order (see
Weiler 1995; Curtin 1997; Bellamy and Castiglione 1997; Nentwich 1998;
Follesdal and Koslowski 1998; Lord 1998a; De Búrca and Scott 2000;
Bellamy and Warleigh 2001).

For such scholars, what is important is not primarily to explain how
the EU has reached its current condition (although this does not mean they
ignore its historical and institutional processes). Instead, the primary task is
to understand and prescribe the means by which the EU's polity-building
process can be accompanied most effectively by a process of democratisation. This is because after the Maastricht Treaty, the EU is clearly a novel
political system of *substantial* power, independence and authority, even if
it is by the same token heavily dependent upon its component parts (the
member states), and of *limited* autonomy. It makes decisions which not
only impact upon EU citizens, but also shift their ability to rely upon
traditional channels of influence to secure their desired outcomes. Citizens
wishing to shape public policy must understand and find ways to influence
the new system, which despite origins in a confederal pact (Forsyth 1981)
has developed *sui generis* properties and structures. Thus, issues of
who controls the processes of integration, how decisions are made, and

how the subjects of the system (EU citizens) relate both to each other and to the decision-making process are of fundamental importance (Chryssochoou 2000).

Models of democracy in the European Union

It remains to sketch the principal theoretical models of the basis for demo-cratisation of the EU, or indeed any transnational organisation: cosmopoli-tanism and communitarianism. Before doing so, however, it would be well to clarify my use of these terms. I follow Brown's (1992: 24–5, 75) usage, in which 'cosmopolitan' and 'communitarian' are terms used to describe schools of thought (rather than rival single theories) at opposite ends of the ideational spectrum in international relations (IR) theory, in an attempt to avoid the more 'loaded' traditional terms (such as 'realism' and 'utopian'). As Brown also says, the use of his terms also helps capture the idea that normative issues are important in IR theory and practice – a notion accepted in many con-temporary studies at the IR/EU studies interface such as the essays in collec-tions edited by Kelstrup and Williams (2000) and Christiansen et al. (1999).

Cosmopolitanism

Cosmopolitan accounts of democracy argue that the interdependence of the contemporary political economy means that it is no longer possible realis-tically to conceive of democracy within one country. This is because no matter how impeccable the nature of democratic practice within any state, the borders of that state are porous in many ways, and it is difficult if not impossible to separate what is international from what is domestic. Because of the existence of many international organisations and regimes which exist to generate public policy, or at least to regulate public life in some way, it is impossible to make policy exclusively within the borders of any country: there is always the need to respond to externally-set agendas/criteria, or, more proactively, to ensure that decisions made 'at home' are not under-mined by opposing decisions made internationally. Multinational companies and stock market operators make decisions which can have a huge impact on a state, but are not necessarily accountable either to it or anyone else except, in the case of multinationals, to their shareholders. Thus, because politics and economics have been internationalised, democracy must be reconfigured in a similar way if any meaningful accountability or partici-pation is to be fostered (Held 1993).

Cosmopolitans argue that democratisation depends on reform of both the state and civil society in order to reflect what might be called the internationalisation imperative. Both governance structures and individual citizens must consciously reorient themselves towards the global level of politics. As a side-benefit, tensions between nation states are likely to reduce, since their power and scope of action would be constrained by regional and global norms, rules and institutions (Held 1993: 43). For cosmopolitans,[11] the essence of democracy is the exercise of universal rights, hence equality between all citizens regardless of (national/ethnic) origin. However, it is important to recognize that there are both maximalist and minimalist cosmopolitans: those who support some kind of social democratic variant of global governance, and those who favour a more neoliberal global polity dominated by market forces. The former argue that we are all bound by our participation in the emerging international legal, economic and security orders to acknowledge and seek where necessary to improve these orders, and thus our sense of solidarity must be global rather than local/national/regional.[12] World government is an ultimate aim of some, but not all, of these scholars. The neoliberal cosmopolitans adopt a minimalist, less redistributive approach, seeking instead to secure a uniform area of free trade.

However, for even maximalist cosmopolitans, what often counts as the ultimate political value is not democracy as such (at least in terms of public participation in, and control of, decision making), but rather the promotion of human rights and public welfare. Democracy may, or may not, be the best means of guaranteeing this: should a majority vote in any polity generate a regime which has a negative impact on either rights or welfare, then other mechanisms of rule (such as recourse to the judiciary or the use of regulatory agencies) may be preferred (Ferrajoli 1996). Thus, there is a contradiction at the heart of cosmopolitanism: it is essentially progressive (in the sense that its maximalist wing promotes social-democratic, 'modernising' values), but it is not necessarily either ultimately democratic or extensive in its aims for a global polity.

Communitarianism

Communitarians have a very different view of what constitutes (international) democracy. For this group of scholars, human rights, as a universal consideration, are of limited number and salience. In essence, what makes rights substantive is their articulation by specific individuals and groups, within a specific culture (Miller 1995). Different groups and societies will differ about whether a given principle is important, and if so, in what way and to what extent – for example, equal treatment of women or homosexuals. Thus, participation in, and belonging to, a given community is the source of what gives an individual her/his meaningful rights and the ability to enact them (Walzer 1994). What counts is not the link between the individual and humankind, but rather the links between the individual and other members of a specific group with which (s)he identifies, and by whom (s)he is recognised as a member.

For most communitarian theorists, the ultimate idea of the community is to be found in nationalism, and the allied view that the nation state is the most effective means of political organisation devised so far (Brown 1992: 71). (Regional nationalists such as the Basques qualify this by arguing that they are nations without states). It is nationality which allows citizens with the necessary shared set of understandings, cultural practices or *Weltanschauung*, which in turn permits them to make mutually comprehensible and justifiable decisions, and then act upon them (Walzer 1983). Communitarians argue that this is the key to democracy: if rights come into conflict (for example, the right of women to control their own reproduction, and the right to life of the unborn), it is only within a given community that acceptable decisions about how to balance those rights can be made. Different communities may make different decisions: without the guiding and supportive *Weltanschauung*, there is no way to guarantee a public decision which will be considered legitimate by those it binds, especially if their personal views are in opposition to the decision. In communitarian eyes, that which constitutes a fundamental criterion of democracy – mutual respect, and acceptance of minority rights by the majority – is guaranteed only by a sense of community. This is because the same mechanism ensures that solidarity and reciprocity can be taken as read and that, as argued by some scholars, within a community we are prepared to make sacrifices for each other that we would not make for outsiders.

There are different kinds of communitarians, just as there are different cosmopolitans. Some communitarians accept only ethnic definitions of community – such as the National Front, or Serbs under the Milosevic regime responsible for 'ethnic cleansing' in the former Yugoslavia. Most, however, reject this view in favour of a more civic perspective which, while not necessarily divorced from ethnic concepts of identity entirely, privileges a vision of community based on the shared understandings of a group of people who have shared territory, culture and language over time – a good example of this is the Gaullists in France. What unites communitarian scholars, however, is a sense that democracy is the ultimate political value. This is because, for communitarians, democracy can only be meaningful when it is operated by, through and for a 'demos' (or people) who consider themselves to be conjoined by shared fate and responsibility. Not only does this sense of community enable the generation of solidarity, it also makes possible the creation of meaningful political debate about what should constitute public policy through a process of deliberation. Communitarians do not suppose that everyone within a community will think alike; they do however, suppose that it is community which enables individuals who disagree to reach a mutually satisfactory settlement of their differences by discussion rather than either force or bargaining (which produces suboptimal outcomes).

Views of democratising the EU

It should be obvious from the above that the two schools of thought have different views of how the EU could, or should, be democratised. To simplify: minimalist cosmopolitans tend to consider the EU to be most democratic as an unfettered free market; maximalist cosmopolitans favour a more 'social' EU, but also favour the further empowerment of the ECJ as well as the European Court of Human Rights (rather than public deliberation) as the main means of ensuring that the EU respects principles of good governance (Van Parijs 1998). For all cosmopolitans though the EU is only a half-way house between nation state and global polity; it is a step in the right direction, but real democratisation is only possible at the global level. Extreme communitarians argue that there is no meaningful sense in which the EU can be made democratic, since a transnational organisation can never have the requisite cultural and ethnic basis. Moderate communitarians argue that a civic European identity is conceivable, but highly unlikely, because although all (national) identities are constructed, and so artificial, they are also very powerful, and likely to resist being subsumed in a European identity (Miller 1995). For both types of communitarian then the EU is always likely to suffer from a democratic deficit: it may be necessary to secure the best use of national sovereignty, but it can never expect to generate affective commitment from individuals, only instrumental use by them as they see fit. All legitimate power, in this view, remains in the hands of the national governments, who have only 'loaned', or delegated, it to the Union.

There is difficulty in adopting either cosmopolitanism or communitarianism if we want to generate a model of how the EU could be democratised; the former group of theorists see the Union as helpfully capable of transcending ethnicity and increasing the common good, but ultimately consider it short of (although perhaps a part of) the ideal (global governance). By definition, this cannot be the goal of specifically *European* integration. Communitarians signal that democracy is never likely to be achievable in the EU context: this may not mean that the EU should be disbanded, but it does mean that it must be reduced to a minimal role in order to protect democracy where it can exist – at the level of the nation state. Clearly, a model for democratising the EU must find a middle way between both schools of thought (Bellamy and Castiglione 1997, 1998) because as has been discussed above, the Union is a developing regional (not national or global) entity with a sound essential justification, and one which is by the same token neither wholly neoliberal nor deeply solidaristic in either maximalist cosmopolitan or the two communitarian variants. It is partially autonomous, and makes a considerable impact upon the lives of its citizens through the provision of public policy. Nonetheless, it cannot rely on a deep sense of community, and it is heavily dependent on its component parts, the member states, for its resources, and, in part, its legitimacy. Although its powers and partial autonomy necessitate that its governance must be accountable and transparent, grounded in political equality, it is not easy to identify the necessary reserves of community upon which it could draw in order to allow this. The goal of the next chapter is to provide a theoretical model which is capable of pointing a way forward by taking the rather messy Union of today as a normative good and setting out how a deliberative theory of democracy can create the framework for a democratic, if unusual, mode of European governance based on the common pursuit of solutions to shared problems rather than a deep sense of shared identity.

NOTES

1   Political legitimacy is perhaps best defined by Beetham and Lord (1998: 15), who argue that it comprises legality (acting within the law), normative justifiability (reflecting general beliefs about the rightful sources and use of authority), and legitimation (receipt of authorisation from those bound by the system, as well as approval by other external authorities which are generally considered legitimate – a form of peer approval).

2   The first pillar is the European Community, comprising matters of the single market and measures already in the EU remit before the Maastricht Treaty such as social policy, environmental policy, and, albeit in a different institutional configuration, the common agricultural policy. Pillar 2 is the common foreign and security policy. Pillar 3 covers matters of police and judicial cooperation (initially called justice and home affairs). The nature and content of these pillars is not static. However, the main significance of the pillar structure is that in only the first pillar do the EU institutions have their full range of powers; in pillars 2 and 3, intergovernmentalism is clearly the dominant mode of decision-making.

3   This is not to imply that the EU is 'only' a market. However, economic integration has so far outpaced the political equivalent, notwithstanding current progress in pillars 2 and 3. Moreover, it is a common strategy for both political and legal actors and institutions to justify proposals or rulings on the grounds that they are necessary to preserve the single market. Such was famously the case of Delors' proposal of the 'European social model', for example.

4   I argue in Chapter 2 that this is no bad thing, and indeed that given the Union's multiple sources of legitimacy it is the optimal developmental method for the integration process. However, there is no doubt that such a deliberative process, if confined to elites, lacks transparency.

5 See Chapter 6 for an in-depth exploration of these issues.

6 As stated above, it is important not to confuse the project of generating an EU-centric identity with cultural discussions of what is, or might be, considered a 'European' identity, given that not all European countries are, or are in some cases likely in the near future to be, members of the EU. Thus, when I use the term 'Europeanisation' of identity I refer to a process by which it is made to take on an element of EU-centricity not a process by which people of non-European cultures adopt European culture or customs.

7 One of the reasons why neofunctionalism was criticised was its very close links with the European integration project, which at times came perilously close to advocacy rather than objective study (Harrison 1974) and also meant that it suffered from excessive reliance on one case study (the 'n = 1' problem) (Rosamond 2000a, 2000b).

8 For an excellent, book-length discussion of European integration theory, see Rosamond (2000a).

9 For useful discussions of the inadequacies of orthodox integration theory, as well as some of the attempts to supersede it, see Warleigh (1998a, 2000a).

10 For an exception, see the work of Moravcsik (1991, 1993, 1999). Moravcsik's liberal intergovernmentalist approach is a sophisticated refinement of inter-governmentalism, rather than a break with it.

11 The following paragraphs draw on Bellamy and Warleigh (1998: 457–63).

12 The term 'regional' is used here in its international relations form, to indicate a region of the globe rather than a unit of governance below the level of the state.

2

Bringing Functionalism Back In: Critical Deliberativism, Liberal Democracy and The Democratic Deficit

The functional-ideational gap: can one size fit all?

One of the difficulties of designing a democratic reform strategy for the EU is the implications of a very simple, but often overlooked fact: the non-state condition of the Union, which is a multi-level transnational polity characterised by variation in its policy regimes and institutional structures. Understanding the need for democratic reform is simple enough; inventing and applying the right formula is another matter entirely. In any case democratisation is not reducible to the establishment of the 'right' institutions: institutions need to change over time to reflect changing contexts, and popular participation and socialisation are also vital since it is in the interplay between structure and agency (i.e. institutions, practices and the uses to which they are put by actors) that democratic transnational governance is possible (on structure and agency in international politics, see Wendt 1987, 1999). In the case of the EU, matters are yet more complex because conventional Western ideas about what constitutes democracy are bound up with ideas of statehood and demos in ways which the EU is, at least currently, unable to match (Armand and Drancourt 1970; W. Wallace 1990; Kohler-Koch 2000).

There is a gap between the practices of the EU and the ideational basis of orthodox democratic governance. As Jachtenfuchs et al. (1998: 433) put it, 'the enormous development of the Europolity both in terms of its institutional structure and its impact has left domestic actors rather unimpressed at least in their ways of conceptualizing legitimate European governance'. Many political actors and commentators have simply been unable to respond to the challenge of democratising a political system which is strong and growing, but also extremely diverse (both institutionally and culturally) and rooted in its component states. In short, most views of how to democratise the EU are reducible to conferring upon it the condition of statehood, and thus applying conventional principles of liberal democracy at the Union level (Warleigh 2002b). Accordingly, they are supported by federalists, opposed by defenders of national sovereignty, and aspired to by many actors in the EU institutions who see in democratisation the ability to enhance either their own powers or at least those of their institutions. In fact, a new kind of polity such as the evolving EU requires a different kind of democratic practice from that practiced in nation states, albeit one that is both deep and enduring (Lord 1998a).

There are further complications, including the existence of different traditions and political cultures in the member states (Jachtenfuchs et al. 1998). Although this diversity does not rule out the evolution of common rules and practices, it does indicate that developing an agreement about what democratisation should entail will be difficult, because any given strategy of democratic reform will be considered differently in the various member states, not just because of the perceived acceptability of its 'challenge' to national sovereignty, but because the different traditions and systems of the various member states are likely to shape public reactions to the same proposal in different ways. States (and citizens) may agree, for example, that a single currency is a good idea, but disagree on the best regime for its pursuit and management. Alternatively, they may disagree fundamentally on the desirability of the euro, and this may be on grounds of national sovereignty or because other ways to achieve the same objective (price stability and economic growth) are preferred. These differences cannot be wished away or expected to change as the result of a Pauline conversion to 'true Europeanism'; instead, they must be accepted as part of the process of polity-building in the EU. Thus, democratisation of the Europolity requires an acceptance that one size currently does not, and may not ever, fit all.

The argument of this chapter, and indeed of this book, is that a solution to the problem of how to democratise the EU can be found if two steps are taken: an acknowledgement that Monnet's[1] fusion of functionalism and federalism was miscalculated, and the subsequent application of what I call a *critical deliberativist*, rather than a liberal, model to the development of democratic politics in the EU. The abuse of functionalist thinking as a strategy of state-building by the EU's founders has created a situation in which the popular response to the democratic deficit has not been an acceptance of democratisation-through-federation, but rather intense criticism of the entire integration project. Given this situation of backlash – unmerited as concerns the essential purpose of the EU, often unjustified in terms of particular issues, but wholly deserved in terms of the democratic credentials of the overall integration strategy – any attempt to impose a federal structure is likely to add to rather than remove the EU's problems of democratic legitimacy. Instead, it is necessary to return to the functionalist view of integration as a set of 'instances where like interests meet and combine into functionally and territorially diversified "clusters of cooperation"' (Tuytschaever 1999: 252) in which divergent views of what the integration process should do or create are not only tolerated, but taken as an essential feature.

As I make clear below, deliberative democracy privileges the socialisation process rather than simply the building of formal institutions: it allows for the creation of popular engagement with, and deeper support for, the European integration process while giving centrality to the management of difference rather than the construction (or simple assumption) of sameness. It seeks to create a substantive rather than merely formal kind of democracy, taking as a central objective the creation of further cross-border solidarity and identification between EU citizens. Such a model is therefore compatible with a deeper and more closely bound EU – something which is likely to be necessary in order to meet the challenges of further enlargement and integration in policy areas such as civil liberties and defence – but has no necessary link to the creation of a Euro-state. Critical deliberation allows different outcomes to the integration process for the various member states and publics, and argues that this is democratically sound rather than the function of intransigent elite behaviour. It is compatible with flexible integration, and sits well with the contemporary Zeitgeist while avoiding a deterministic view that any given difference, policy regime or policy style should remain unchanging, or that any given configuration of institutions and practices of governance should remain unaltered over time.

However, there are certain issues which must be squarely confronted if we are to apply critical deliberativism. First, attention should be paid here to the word 'critical': like any theoretical model, deliberativism contains weaknesses which must be addressed if it is to be translatable to real-world politics. Thus, in this chapter I seek to establish a version of deliberativism which is capable of harnessing some of the benefits of liberal democracy (such as the use of adjudicative and representative mechanisms when necessary) while avoiding its weaknesses with particular regard to the EU. This is not simply for strategic reasons, following the argument that forms of democracy which bear a resemblance to existing norms and practices are more likely to appear attractive to both citizens and political elites as they require less of a rupture with the present 'ideational frame' (Kohler-Koch 2000; Schmitter 1998, 2000). It is also because, at a normative level, liberal democracy has certain features which are worth preserving, at least insofar as they set a baseline against which other forms of democracy must be judged (Macpherson 1977).

Second, it is necessary to acknowledge that any form of deliberative democracy requires active participation by citizens. I assume that current popular dissatisfaction with the way the EU works reflects a wish to play a greater part in the governance of the Union, even if further socialisation is necessary in order to provide the skills and knowledge to do this success-fully. It is possible that this is not the case, and that perceptions of a demo-cratic deficit in the EU owe more to general alienation and apathy than could be countered by almost any reform of the Union. If this is true then a Schumpeterian form of democracy concentrating almost solely on struc-tures and paternalism would be both more suitable and easier to put into place, requiring only the creation of partisan governance in the Council and elections of national representatives to it (even indirectly by national parliaments). It would do less to solve the root causes of the problem, but it could suffice to create a mechanism for 'throwing the rascals out', or at least more overt patterns of coalition/consensus formation in Council, and thereby give a democratic veneer to the provision of bread and circuses.

Third, deliberativist democracy requires the rejection of the idea that the EU should, or must, end up as a state, whether unitary or (more likely) federal, even though there is nothing in deliberative democracy which precludes the eventual creation of such a state by either a group or the ensemble of the member states if that is their collective will. Deliberative democracy merely takes it as a given that such an outcome is not the neces-sary goal of integration, and treats as a normative good worth preserving (and revising) the current rather messy condition of the integration process in all its multi-level, variegated complexity (Bellamy and Warleigh 1998). Such may be a step beyond many advocates of integration, whose ideational frames are too closely wedded to federalism: the Governance White Paper put forward by the Commission in 2001, as well as the difficulties of secur-ing Commission and EP support for an operationalisable form of flexibility (Warleigh 2002a), indicate that such ideational renewal will not be easy.

In the next section I examine the reasons why the Monnet-style marriage of functionalism and federalism has proved so problematic. In the following section I show why, despite its inclusion of certain worthy prin-ciples and practices, liberal democracy is unsuitable as a model for the democratisation of the EU on both strategic and normative counts as a result of its links to a project of state-building at the EU level. Finally, I discuss the theory of deliberative democracy and set out the elements of a functionalist/critical deliberativist model of democratic reform in the EU.

Strategies of building EU democracy: federalist or functionalist?[2]

As demonstrated in the previous chapter issues of democracy were not high on the agenda of the EU's founders – at least, not in any direct sense. However, the principal tension of the integration process – the perceived duty to balance national sovereignty with the needs of the joint policy-making system by which it was exercised – certainly was. The roots and design of the EU both lie in this balancing act, for the principal architect of what is now the EU, Jean Monnet, sought to provide the necessary balance by using quasi-functionalist means to achieve federalist ends (Featherstone 1994; Holland 1994). Monnet's approach was to build a European federation gradually; perturbed by the weakness of the institutions of joint European governance set up in the immediate aftermath of the Second World War (which were firmly controlled by national governments), and convinced for the same reason that political will to generate a European federation was lacking, Monnet proposed the step-by-step integration of Europe. Starting with a key policy area (coal and steel industries) in which international agreement to share power could be found, integration would progress incrementally until eventually it had created a European state in all but name.

The contribution of this strategy to the democratic deficit was established in Chapter 1, and need not be reiterated at length here. However, it is necessary to explain the theoretical underpinnings of federalism and functionalism in order to establish why, at a conceptual level, this attempted balance is misconceived. Before doing so, however, it is worth explaining in more detail why Monnet and his fellow founders of the EU were obliged to take up this strategy – that is, why it was impossible to create a federal United States of Europe at the outset of the integration process, but also why pressures for integration of a deeper nature than had previously been attempted were capable of being harnessed to this novel project.

The impossibility of federalism

At the end of the Second World War it was clear that cooperation between European countries was necessary for economic recovery, and also that some new kind of military alliance which involved the USA was vital (initially to ensure the peace of the continent, and subsequently to protect its Western half against the USSR-led Eastern half). This led to the creation of important organisations such as the Organisation for European Economic Cooperation (set up to administer the Marshall Plan funds, and later re-named the Organisation for Economic Cooperation and Development– OECD) and NATO. Significantly, these organisations included important non-European states: the USA and Canada.[3] However, for several sets of reasons, neither at the end of the war nor in the decades immediately after was there sufficient support for the creation of a federal state in Europe at either mass or elite levels.

First, there was insufficient pressure from the most powerful states which held a stake in European stability in the immediate post-war world – the USA, the USSR and (at least for a short time) the UK. Neither of the then-superpowers consistently sought to establish a European federation. The USA was not necessarily opposed to the idea, and indeed many important actors in the US foreign policy community considered that it was the logical choice for a continent in need of economic integration as well as guaranteed peace (Dinan 1999:17). However, although the USA offered much-needed financial aid to the European states through the 1947 Marshall Plan, and insisted that the recipient states must cooperate in its implementation, it did not insist on the creation of a United States of Europe in the face of opposition from the two most powerful West European states of the day – the UK and France (Hobsbawm 1994). Instead, as a central plank of its strategy for post-war pre-eminence, Cold War diplomacy and greater prosperity, the US gave its support to other forms of European cooperation in which it played an official role as participant rather than merely sponsor, and indeed, in the case of NATO, clearly as first among equals. The role of the USA in supporting and shaping European integration to this day cannot be underestimated (W. Wallace 1997); but equally, it must not be misrepresented as a continual pressure for a European federation, a goal which has been both supported and opposed by US foreign policy at different times (Weigall and Stirk 1992).

The USSR perceived no interest in a post-war European federation, above all because the latter was seen to be a covert means by which the US could, if permitted, extend its influence into countries included in the Soviet sphere of influence at Yalta. Worse, even if confined to the Western half of the continent, integration could set up a potential rival power to the USSR. The strong security rationale for this opposition – the insistence on the division of Germany, the creation of a *cordon sanitaire,* and the control of neighbouring countries which had often caused problems for first Russian, then Soviet security (Dawisha 1990) – was coupled with an ideological equivalent. Although most of the nominally autonomous countries of Central and Eastern Europe had very little independence as part of the USSR's empire-cum-buffer zone – witness the military quashing of reform movements in Hungary (1956) and the then-Czechoslovakia (1968)[4] – it is also true that successive leaders of the USSR derived part of their domestic legitimacy from claims to be at the head of a fraternity (sic) of nations which would be the vanguard of a new communist world order (Dawisha 1990:11).[5] Thus, the Soviet Union had little to gain from supporting the idea of European federalism, although as the Cold War deepened, the USSR can be said to have contributed indirectly to European integration in the Western half of the continent by providing an enemy against whom it was considered necessary to unite under the protection of the US. By the same token, the USSR came to accept the integration process as part of the status quo which enabled it to dominate its 'half' of Europe while the superpowers played out their conflict in other areas of the globe.

Despite much pro-integration rhetoric from its war-time leader Winston Churchill, the United Kingdom was at best ambivalent about the desirability of such an entity as a federal European state (Young 1998). For most UK politicians at the close of the Second World War, European integration in matters other than free trade had symbolic importance but was unlikely to succeed; federation was certainly a project in which the UK could have no role given the required sacrifice of national sovereignty. Ultimately, however, the integration project was to be encouraged if it made 'the continent' stable and thereby allowed the UK to achieve strategic importance as the crucial link between the USA, the Commonwealth, and Europe. Arguably, by its aloof stance the UK did much to endanger the integration projects of the 1950s, because the Benelux countries sought UK participation in the European Coal and Steel Community (ECSC) as a counterweight to French influence, and had severe misgivings about their own participation without the UK (Dinan 1999). Britain's reluctant accession to the EU in 1973 owes as much to an admission that it had miscalculated the possibilities for success of the integration process as to an exaggeration of the UK's ability to remain prosperous on the outside.[6]

A second, and perhaps even more crucial, factor was that those states which participated in the post-war European institutions, and even those which agreed to join the predecessor of the EU, the European Coal and Steel Community of 1952, did so not out of federal zeal but as a means of securing the national interest (Milward 1994; Moravcsik 1999). During the Second World War, bolstered by both left-wing ideas of internationalism and hard-learned lessons about the dangers of extreme nationalism, the popularity of federalism grew; many of those in war-time Resistance movements in several countries had very strong attachments to the idea of a European federation as the means to resuscitate the continent (Urwin 1992: 7). However, not many of those who had been active in the war-time Resistance movements became leaders of their countries after the war ended; instead, with the uniting strand of a struggle against a common enemy dissolved, the internally diverse Resistance movements splintered and the reins of power were often taken up by former leaders returning from exile or those under their tutelage. These actors' views on integration were far more instrumental, and less idealistic, than those in the Resistance (Urwin 1992: 7–12). France sought to ensure that German economic and industrial recovery would not lead to its own eclipse, either militarily or economically; Germany sought its political rehabilitation on terms that would be acceptable to France as well as the UK and the USA (Weigall and Stirk 1992: Ch. 4). The Benelux countries sought economic growth and a boost to their own nascent, but struggling economic union (Schmitt 1962;

W. Wallace 1997: 30); Italy sought a solution to its unemployment problem through enhanced possibilities for labour migration (Schmitt 1962).

The third factor was that there was no clamouring for a European federation at popular level which could have provided the basis for a bold leader or set of leaders to seize the day. In addition to the dissipation of the Resistance and its pro-federal loyalties, there was the deliberate re-focusing of the popular imagination on the idea and structure of the nation state by national elites (Milward 1994). Thus, federalists had no solid source of support on which to draw, and most of those in positions of power routinely opposed their ideas about the shape European integration should take, even if they supported other forms of European cooperation.

Federalism and functionalism: theoretical bases

Consequently those seeking to create a European federation had to search for means other than the proclamation of a new superstate with a new constitution – at least initially. Within the European integration movement, two rival theories of how the process could best be effectuated were in evidence: as well as federalism (in both immediate and gradualist variants), functionalism also had its adherents. It would be wrong to assume that these two theories, or their supporters, always sat well together (Navari 1996); indeed, the argument of this chapter is precisely that the corruption of the second in the pursuit of the first lies at the heart of the EU's democracy problem. Nonetheless, it is important to realise the coexistence of, and differences between, the two theories within the movement, in order subsequently to explain how and why Monnet's strategy was elaborated, and why it managed to gain acceptance.

Historically, federalist projects for European unity have often been used as a cover for imperialism, i.e. the justification of empire-building as the guarantee of peace. A case in point is St. Pierre's 18th century *Projet de la Paix Perpétuelle*, which advocated French hegemony by another name. As stated above, 20th century federalists have tended to be more authentically non-nationalistic. However, federalist approaches to European integration have tended to be political rather than strictly academic, emanating from advocates of federal governance seeking political goals rather than from a clear academic school of thought (Rosamond 2000a: 23). Clearly, this does not make federalism an invalid approach to international governance; however, it does make its academic evaluation more difficult.

In terms of international relations rather than comparative politics, federalism is a theory of securing the peace between states by subsuming them in a new, larger state (albeit not necessarily a global one). With roots in the philosophy of thinkers such as Kant, federalists have a long history and can rightly claim distinction for the perception that domestic policy problems are unlikely to be solved in a climate of international hostility. States preparing for, or prosecuting, war are not able to concentrate on domestic issues sufficiently; states not directly involved in conflict are nonetheless constrained by it, given the disruptions to international trade and the potential for conflict to stretch beyond its initial location to involve more states. Caught in a cycle of constant preparation for, or participation in, war, states have a reduced ability to secure, and interest in, the welfare of their citizens in day-to-day matters: the more powerful states seek to defend their power and resources, while their less powerful neighbours alternately seek to avoid conflict, or, upon perception of possibly momentary opportunity, to pursue their own advantage in the hope of changing the pecking order. Thus, in terms of Kantian federalism, in order to secure peace and increase public welfare the system of separate states must be replaced by reform at both domestic and international levels. Domestically, states must adopt a strict separation of powers to reduce the likelihood of tyrannical centralised rule; internationally there must be an overarching legal system complemented by voluntary federations of the newly reorganised states (Williams et al. 1993, Ch. 9).

European federalists advocate above all the creation of a new supranational state, based on a new constitution and a clear separation of powers between the new centre and periphery. As King (1982) argues, although all states must have some kind of balance between centre and periphery, the distinguishing feature of federalism is that this balance is constitutionally prescribed (and thus changeable only by mutual consent of actors at both levels): territorial representation based on a binding compact is the key principle of federal governance. There is no single pattern in this allocation of power; some federal systems are more centralised than others, giving federalism a useful elasticity which sits oddly with its otherwise prescriptive and legalistic orientation. Federalists are divided, however, on the issue of whether the creation of new federal structures can predate a supporting popular consensus. For Hodges (1978: 241), the dominant thinking in federalism is that the key to creating the new state is securing sufficient political will at the elite level; the masses will eventually accept the new structures as a result of their demonstrated benefits even if they are initially opposed to them. Thus, although many federalists may seek ultimately to create a new demos or people for the new superstate, they privilege the establishment of institutions as a first step in this process. Alternatively, they may see the creation of a European federation as the means by which citizens wake up to the supposed existence of their shared 'European moral identity' based on Christianity and Charlemagne (Siedentop 2000: 194–203). According to Rosamond (2000a: 25–9), however, it is important to acknowledge that certain federalists – of both academic and practitioner kinds – have advocated a different view, namely that prior popular interaction is vital as the basis for an understanding of the necessity for, and practice of, federal governance. In this kind of federalism, gradualism may be preferred to the constitutional 'big bang' approach; although both kinds of federalist see the necessary outcome as a new superstate, they differ about the best method to achieve this outcome, given the need to secure support at both elite and popular levels. As a consequence the European movement has been divided between the two schools of thought (gradualism versus the 'big bang' approach) (Holland 1994; Navari 1996).

Functionalism, on the other hand, is a theory of how peace can best be preserved by promoting interdependence between states and locking them into sectoral policy regimes.[7] For functionalists, European integration must not be about the construction of a new state/federation; instead, peace is considered to be preserved most effectively by promoting and then cementing interdependence through a system of international agencies, each devoted to a specific policy area. Deep and sustained cooperation by states (which become dependent on each other to create and deliver their policies) is necessary to avoid conflict between them, but the creation of a new superstate is seen as at best unlikely and at worst as merely ratcheting up the problem of territorial division to a new level. Functionalists argue that states (or at least those who hold power in them) are unlikely to destroy the status quo by abdicating national sovereignty (and thus, at least a significant degree of their power); instead, those seeking to promote integration or international cooperation are better advised to create a means by which state power is truncated (or shared) in reality, even if not rhetorically.

For functionalists, the key reason why international conflict happens is because we have created and perpetuated the idea of social organisation through the device of the supposedly independent state, which should be recognised as an artificial construct, i.e. as one tool among many by which social life is, or might be, regulated, rather than an inevitable necessity. Although the use of the state to organise social life can lead to efficiency and increased welfare, this cannot be taken for granted. Indeed, Mitrany (1933, 1975) argued that in the face of what we would now call globalisation, states have become both oppressive and redundant: oppressive in the sense that domestically they have a role in an ever increasing number of areas which are properly located in the private sphere, and redundant in that economic interdependence has reduced national rulers' abilities to promote or defend their citizens' interests. States also create false divisions between people because, put simply, a border is erected at a given geographical point to divide 'us' from 'them', often for no other reason than the fact that that point represents the historical limits of a ruler's ability to use coercive power effectively. Moreover, the division of the world into separate states leads to a mindset in which state rulers consider that their prime directive is preservation of the state by means fair or foul, and an international system which is correspondingly 'anarchic' (Camilleri and Falk 1992).

Thus, in the functionalist model of international integration, what is important is to take a gradual approach, but not a state- or federation-building one. Nation states exist, and cannot be wished away; instead, it is necessary to reduce their capacity for use as instruments of war by slowly but steadily increasing the number and degree of interdependencies between them. Economic interdependence was a starting point to be complemented by a series of structures of international governance, each devoted to a (set of) functional task(s). Division in political life would be by policy area, not territory; political authority would rest with the citizens of the globe in terms of system-shaping ('constitutional') decisions, and with the sectoral agencies in matters of daily policy. Each sectoral agency would be account-able to a sectoral parliament, with disputes between them adjudicated by both an international judiciary and a special body elected by a world con-gress (Mitrany 1933, 1971; Hancock 1941/4[8]).

The precise structure and tasks of each agency would alter over time; no state would be compelled to take part in every agency, but interdepen-dence would make the participation of most states in most agencies likely over time. Conflicts would be solved by negotiation rather than imposed solutions whenever possible and this negotiated, deliberative approach would supplement increasing interdependence to create a deeper sense of international community over time. However, it would not guarantee the production of any given form of international organisation; the changing patterns of cooperation should be left to evolve over time, within the frame of 'policing' by the international judiciary and related bodies. Moreover, functionalists argued that international cooperation was above all a politi-cal process, ultimately dependent upon both public support and an ongoing process of contested (i.e. publicly debated), gradualism (Warleigh 2002b, Ch. 2). Public support would be guaranteed by the maximisation of public welfare and a role for the citizen in decision-making; contestation would ensure that no state was compelled to enter into an agency with which it disagreed, or at least would give it a stake in shaping that agency (Hancock 1941/4). The development of the system would be fostered by a certain degree of activism on the international level, a gradual shift in ideational frame at both popular and elite levels, and, to a degree, a kind of domino effect created by states' perceived need to keep up with each other: once an agency had been created, states would usually consider their interests to be best served by participation in it rather than staying outside, as a result of cost-benefit calculation rather than changed ideational framework if need be (Mitrany 1975).

Monnet's strategy: federalism through functionalism

It can be seen that at a certain level there are similarities between gradualist federalism and functionalism. Both consider the existence of separate states to be a major contributor to international conflict and instability, and both consider that for that reason states should have their capacity to wage war removed by their reinvention as part of a binding international system. Furthermore, both theories consider that the means to achieve this objective must not be narrowly economic, but also political (in the sense that it must be a public enterprise and involve both top-down elements of institution-building and bottom-up processes of socialisation).

Given this similarity, it must have seemed that functionalism could supply an indication of the means by which gradualist federalism could be maintained, by giving it a mechanism through which the process could be kept in perpetual motion: the functionalists' idea of the domino-effect of sectoral integration, which neofunctionalists devoted to the study of the EU later gave centrality as the concept of 'spillover' (Haas 1968, 1964). However, it must be recognised that these similarities were more apparent than real. Functionalists' perception of the means, objectives and desired end-product of international integration were wholly different from those of even gradualist federalists because they did not focus on the creation of a new regional state, either normatively or practically (Mitrany 1965). Monnet's use of a highly elitist variant of functionalist methods (Navari 1996) to secure federalist goals was not ultimately capable of success, because functionalism's basic rationale is that states will only give up/share/pool their sovereignty if they do not fear what Pentland (1973: 124) calls their 'self-abnegation' in a new state. Given that the creation of such a structure was Monnet's ultimate goal, it should not have been expected that functionalist methods could be of use.

It should be emphasised here that Monnet was not attempting to create a coherent theory of European integration, but rather a practical strategy by which federalism could be taken further than the OEEC and Council of Europe were able. His immediate need was to establish an elite coalition of support in a sufficient number of states (Holland 1994). His proposal of the ECSC was, on this level, inspired. It brought Franco-German reconciliation much closer, and involved key areas of both policy (coal and steel production, at the time the key to both industrial and military rejuvenation) and territory – notably the areas of the Franco-German border. It presented other European states with useful benefits, even if the UK's non-participation caused worries in certain quarters (see above). It vested most power in the High Authority, the predecessor of the Commission, providing an institution with both the capacity to lead the integration process and an institutional interest in so doing. Monnet's plan had demonstrable utility for national governments. It was also credible for federalists to assume that it could set in train an ongoing process of integration, given the importance of the policy sectors involved. Although Monnet did not secure the support of the entire European movement (Murray 1996), he was able to rely upon that of the gradualist federalists, and appeared to have designed a 'win-win' way forward for what federalists had perceived to be a stalling process of post-war integration.

However, Monnet's strategy did not achieve its main goal. It is true that the ECSC set out an institutional structure which was both obviously supranational in nature and the blueprint for that of the present-day EU (Dinan 1999), although that structure has been modified in many important ways since the 1950s (Warleigh 2001e). Nonetheless, although the Community Method has had a lasting impact on the way the integration process works, it has not brought about a European federation, or even a federal union of those member states which began the process. Instead, member states have been as alive to the perceived federalising potential of the chosen strategy since its inception as Monnet was himself, and have collectively blocked it on many occasions. Within the negotiations for the ECSC itself, Monnet was forced to accept the addition of the Council of Ministers to the institutional framework, thereby introducing a clear intergovernmental element (Dinan 1999). In 1954, the proposal for a European Defence Community, the next initiative based on Monnet's strategy, was not ratified; thus, within two years the limits of his strategy were clear. In 1957, the European Economic Community and the European Atomic Community were agreed, reinvigorating the integration process. However, two major points must be made here. First, both the new communities were created as a means of promoting economic, rather than political, integration (Forsyth 1981; Moravcsik 1999). Second, the member states reversed the balance of power between the Council of Ministers and the High Authority/Commission; the scope of European integration might thus increase, but its ultimate control would lie in the hands of the participant governments, even if they agreed that their interests were better served by a set of EU institutions with a degree of autonomous power and the ability to protect/promote the common interest when necessary (Forsyth 1981).

Step-changes in the integration process such as the SEA and TEU are thus attributable not solely, or even primarily, to spillover, but rather to intergovernmental bargains in the face of domestic and international pressures (Sandholtz and Zysman 1989; Pryce, 1994). As I argue elsewhere, this does not mean that national governments are the only important actors in the integration process (Warleigh 2000a, 2000b, 2001a), or that there are limits to the scope of the integration process which can be defined a priori (Warleigh 1998). Neither does it mean that member states always make 'rational' decisions and face no important constraints or problems as a result of previous decisions – there is clearly a sense in which 'path dependency' is an important factor in EU decision making (Pierson 1996). It *does* mean, however, that member states are unlikely to find themselves involuntarily trapped in a federal state of the Commission's – or anybody else's – making.

Monnet's strategy had another highly significant lasting impact, however, namely the idea that the EU should be considered a state-in-waiting whose democratisation could lie only in the application of the dominant view of legitimate state-based governance, liberal democracy (Warleigh 2002b). Thus, Featherstone (1994) advocates the abandonment of the Community Method in favour of a more traditional liberal democratic state at EU level. In the next section of this chapter I shall argue that for both strategic and normative reasons this approach is erroneous, and in the subsequent section I argue that the Community Method must be abandoned in favour of a critical deliberativist model based more clearly on functionalism.

The inadequacy of liberal democracy: normative issues

Liberal democracy: virtues and outline

The problems inherent in attempting to apply liberal democracy to the case of the Europolity are both normative and strategic. Inevitably, the former conditions the latter: a strategy for reform based on inappropriate conceptual underpinnings is unlikely to succeed. Given that much of the emphasis placed on democracy in EU governance is driven by the need to respond to public disquiet, it is worth setting out clearly why a response to the problem based on the liberal democratic blueprint (LDB) would be mistaken, and what that blueprint is.

As the first step in so doing, however, it is necessary to acknowledge that the LDB exerts a strong pull over the popular imagination for very good reasons. Since it is the dominant strand in Western thinking about what constitutes democracy, it is bound to play a significant role almost by default through a kind of conceptual hegemony (Levine 1981). That said, there is virtue in liberal democracy which must be acknowledged for two principal reasons. First, it sets a standard below which other forms of democracy must not fall if they are to be attractive (Lord and Beetham 2001); second, it contains ideas which are useful and which can help critique other forms of democracy by means of 'creative tension' in the Kuhnian sense. As Macpherson (1977:10) argues, liberal democracy contains a stress on 'actual involvement in joint political action' as the sole means by which 'people (can) transcend their consciousness of themselves as consumers and appropriators'. This emphasis on participation (albeit often in indirect form) and self-consciousness as a political actor is an important part of the liberal democratic tradition; although liberal democracy's current incarnation may emphasise this less than its past avatars, such readings of liberal democracy are not the only possible variants (C. Taylor 1998). In the best tradition of liberalism itself, liberal democracy places importance on individual fulfilment as the rationale for such collective action, thereby giving a convincing reason why individuals should engage with public life.[9]

Liberal democratic thought is perhaps best conceived as a spectrum which ranges from libertarianism minimalism to participatory, if ultimately representative, democracy. It is a school of thought, not a single approach. Its main goals were to prevent the arbitrary use of political power and promote the maximum possible individual freedom within a framework of limited government organised on the basis of representation and the protection of minority rights. Liberal democrats come in different varieties, and liberal democracy developed over time from the thought of philosophers such as Montesquieu, Locke, Bentham and Mill, with more contemporary, and varied, contributions from such thinkers as Rawls, Hayek and Friedman. Thus, there are often significant differences between liberal democratic thinkers to which I cannot do justice here.[10]

I am not going to argue that liberal democracy is reducible to the rule of the market, and thus inherently undemocratic at base. Neither am I going to argue that its precepts of representative, limited government have no value. It is even true that the EU is 'one of the few attempts at creating a new form of political system within a liberal democratic framework' (Andersen and Eliassen 1996: 3), and that liberal democracy therefore has a certain adaptability to politics beyond the level of the (nation) state. However, I *am* going to argue that despite this the LDB is normatively unsuitable for use as a guide to democratic reform of the EU for three main reasons. First, although this criticism can be exaggerated, liberal democracy does lend itself too easily to a subsuming of the political into the economic, and thus to a formal rather than substantive kind of democracy. Second, it relies at base on the existence of a state (even if a federal one) in order to shore itself up, and the EU is not a state despite its powers as a regulator and public policy maker. Third, liberal democracy relies heavily on the existence of a closely bound community/demos, which is simply non-existent in the EU context.

Liberal democracy results from political thought designed to justify state/parliamentary reform and the 'independence of private enterprise from political control' (Sabine 1939: 648). For liberal democrat thinkers, government is something of a necessary evil. Ideally, we would have no (or minimal) public power, but since the 'good life' (understood as the ability of each citizen to pursue her/his own course of action in her/his own way) cannot be assured in a condition of anarchy in which everyone seeks to defend her/his own interests, in all likelihood to the detriment of other people, everyone benefits from some degree of regulation of public life which ensures a degree of mutuality. We may be in the majority today, but in the minority tomorrow; to feel secure while in a minority we need to know that our interests will not be ridden roughshod over by the majority, and need in return to accept such restraint when we form the majority ourselves. Moreover, holding public power is a burden and time-consuming; given the scale of contemporary political structures, direct democracy such as that of the Greek city-states is not feasible, so government must be practiced by a set of actors specially entrusted with that task (elected representatives), whose correct behaviour we ensure by making them subject to laws and removal from office by the means of the ballot. By the same token, public authorities' principal task is to provide stability and balance in the public sphere, in order to ensure the basis on which economic growth can be built. This is to be achieved by creating enduring political structures based on the principles of the rule of law, political equality and free choice of representation, which ensure that although those people in power may change, the institutions and systems remain. Thus, government should be *representative* and *permissive*; liberal democracy has an important pluralist strand insofar as it gives centrality to the idea of *legitimate opposition*.

However, for liberals the emphasis is on the reduction of government/ public power to the minimum necessary level; what counts most is the preservation of individual liberty, which can be truncated insofar as is necessary to ensure the pursuit of self-interest does not harm others unduly, but only to that extent. Functions of government should thus be *limited*. Not all life should be subject to public power; the 'private sphere' of business and family life should have minimal public regulation.[11] Functions of government should also be clearly separated, so that no one set of actors or institution can arrogate too many powers to itself. Public power must be organised alongside an open society, in which an independent judiciary (and a free press) are guaranteed. In essence, a metaphorical bargain is struck between the individual (who agrees to sacrifice a degree of her/his liberty) and the state (which agrees to keep its powers to a minimum); the individual agrees to the existence of public power because she/he benefits from it and knows that if she/he disagrees with a particular public policy she/he can protest against it, and can ultimately replace those in power with other actors should she/he be able to gain sufficient support from others.

Critiques of liberal democracy as a normative model for the EU

The first important critique of the LDB from the perspective of this book is the relationship between politics and economics that it envisages. For many commentators, the LDB is inadequate because its compromise between liberalism and democracy is insufficient, and always likely to privilege economics given its view that government functions should be minimised, their ultimate purpose being to allow stability in order for the successful generation of wealth. This is attributed to the LDB's core principles, which serve to preserve elite privilege through the notion of the protection of minority rights instead of promoting deeper social reform; as Levine puts it, although liberal democracy is a clear advance on its predecessor regimes (autocracies), in absolute terms it is 'overwhelmingly liberal and only very tenuously democratic' (Levine 1981: 7) because its ultimate goal is to secure the conditions necessary for a successful capitalist economy rather than social justice or participatory governance. Thus, although other types of regime can be capitalist, the relationship between liberal democracy and capitalism is 'conceptual, not merely historical' (Levine 1981: 153; see also Fukuyama 1992; Dryzek 1996)[12].

This is linked in turn to liberal democracy's mistrust of politics: in seeking to limit the tasks and powers of government, the LDB creates limits to the use of public power as an instrument of both social change and politicisation of the individual. Aggregate public welfare may be pursued, but elite control of public power is guaranteed; reliance upon representative government may permit change of the actors who compose the elite, but does little to allow individuals real ability to make their views count in the making of public policy, apart from infrequently at the time of elections (Levine 1981: 32). True democracy, it is argued, depends on the use of discourses and practices based not on aggregation of preferences but on ideas other than economic rationality (Dryzek 1996: 146); once established, liberal democratic states are more than capable of evolution, but rarely disturb substantively the fundamental balance struck between liberalism and democracy in favour of the former even if they take on a greater role in public welfare (Dryzek 1996). Thus, if applied to the EU, the LDB would do little to rectify the current imbalance between economic and political integration despite any institutional change.

The second critique is that the LDB relies upon a (Westphalian) state structure for successful elaboration. Liberal democracy was conceived as a matter of transforming public power in a bid to secure the interests of elites and the bourgeoisie by limited extension of the franchise and the establishment of a suitable framework for wealth creation through capitalism. In turn, this framework relies upon the existence of discrete political structures, which each have exclusive control of public power within their borders, the internal monopoly of legitimate violence, a strong bureaucracy which gathers taxes and administers the system, and institutions with the authority and personnel to make binding public decisions (Caporaso 1996: 34–5). Liberal democracy can thus be taken to be inextricably linked to the development of the Western state system in its complex interplay between economic and political forces leading on from the Treaty of Westphalia in 1648, even though its apex was not reached until the mid–late 19th century (for an overview, see Hobsbawm 1997).

As Caporaso (1996) points out, it is true that there are many forms of such states, and that the Westphalian model is more an ideal-type than a reality. It is also true that given contemporary conditions of interdependence the ongoing viability of the Westphalian model has been brought into question on many occasions (Camilleri and Falk 1992; Krasner 1999). However, the point here is that the LDB relies upon such a state for its realisation, and that in the context of the EU no such state exists. It must be remembered that the EU has *member states* which set it up by Treaty and ultimately control its development through a process of Treaty reform (judgments of the ECJ notwithstanding) (Forsyth 1981). Although it could be argued that the Union bears comparison with contemporary forms of the state, such as the regulatory model (Majone 1996) or the postmodern (Ward 1997), both of which have problematic relations with liberal democracy, the Union's resemblance to the liberal democratic version of the Westphalian state is at best shallow, an illusion generated by the existence at EU level of institutions vaguely in keeping with the LDB. The EU has no monopoly of legitimate violence (in fact, it has no ability to use violence within its own borders at all); no ability to raise tax directly; chronic personnel shortages, despite Eurosceptic propaganda to the contrary; and, given the current primacy of non-legislative modes of decision-making in Union governance (H. Wallace 2000), what may even be a decreasing ability to make binding public decisions. Thus, regardless of whether the EU should be considered a state-in-waiting or not, it is clear that it does not currently fit the broad framework of the state necessary for the invocation of the LDB (Bellamy and Castiglione 2000a: 170–4). Moreover, the use of the EU's undoubted public power as a teleological device to acquire that status would do violence to the core tenet of liberal democracy – limited government – even if it would suit the purpose of federalists. Advocates of the LDB as a blueprint for Union democracy must therefore confess to either closet federalism or closet communitarianism (see Chapter 1), since they must seek either to make the EU a Westphalian state or limit democracy to the level at which such states may still – albeit erroneously – be taken to exist (the national level).

Attempting to use liberal democracy as a model for democratic reform of the EU has a further crucial flaw which is somewhat related to the lack of a Union state, but is analytically separate: the non-existence of a European political community/demos (see Chapter 6). Within liberal democracy, a sense of community must be established in order to ensure majority respect for minority rights and identification of the individual with both the political system and the other individuals bound by it. This sense of community – of a group of people who identify each other as part of the same group and who agree to be bound by common rules – is severely lacking at the EU level. As pointed out in Chapter 1, the Union may be accepted by much of the population in the member states as a necessary part of the public policy making process. This does not mean, however, that the majority of member state nationals identify in any significant way with either the Union or nationals of other member states. With further enlargement in prospect, this diversity and lack of mutual identification is set to grow, not diminish (Scharpf 1999: 187). In the absence of such community, liberal democratic institutions are problematic, since without this 'common frame of political reference' member state nationals are likely to consider majoritarian institutions such as the EP illegitimate (Andersen and Eliassen 1996:7; Dryzek 2000: 116).

Advocates of liberal democracy in the EU are in a bind: they are right to point to the importance of the demos in legitimate Union governance, but this actually precludes them from applying their model to the EU. As the EU is composed of liberal democracies, it is difficult for those seeking EU reform to advocate the role of the demos without acknowledging the existence of currently at least 15 *demoi* within the Union system which seem obstinately to prefer identification with subnational or national systems/communities as superior sources of community. As stated above, demos-creation by EU institutions is deeply against the spirit (if not always the practice) of liberal democracy, even if the Union had the necessary capacity and resources to do it. And yet, advocates of the LDB have no other means of generating this sense of Euro-demos, given that 50 years of integration have so far failed to produce significant loyalty transfer by the EU's undoubted provision of public welfare and the generation of wealth. Thus, liberal democracy is an inadequate model for reform of the EU, but in its shortcomings (the general primacy of economics over politics) and in its problems (highlighting the importance of community while being unable to guarantee the mechanism for its generation) it signals issues to be addressed by any more successful model of reform.[13]

The inadequacy of liberal democracy: strategic issues

Beyond Westphalia

Perhaps the most egregious strategic misfit between the LDB and the requirements of democratising the contemporary EU is its assumption of a solid basis for majoritarian politics – the assumption that the EU can be treated as if it were a Westphalian polity with a corresponding demos.

This is because in fact the EU is a polity riven with cleavage across many axes – national, subnational, sectoral, North–South, East–West, cultural/linguistic to name but a few – and thus in fact the necessary form of democracy is one devoted to cleavage management on the basis of a frank admission of these differences (Majone 1996: 286–7).

Strategies for reform based on majoritarianism are likely to perpetuate the EU's problematic legitimacy because they will at best fail to resonate with a public which fails to be aware of them, and at worst cause resentment at being corralled into a synthetic demos; in both cases the gap between federalist aspirations to collective identity and its uncertain existence in the real world is highlighted. (For a discussion with regard to the European Parliament, see Chapter 4.) Moreover such strategies require the upfront sacrifice of too much national sovereignty; most member states are simply not willing to take the steps necessary to create a truly majoritarian system even in the Council, never mind in the rest of the institutional structure. The formal existence of a single EU electorate for EP elections is a useful indicator here: EU citizens can vote and stand in elections to the EP in a member state in which they reside but whose nationality they lack. However, most such citizens do not take up this opportunity (Day and Shaw 2000), and in any case are a relatively small number. Furthermore, member states have refused to create a single electoral system for such elections, or even to agree on a common date for voting. Campaigns are run by national, not European, parties and the importance of such elections is almost universally seen to be at best secondary, despite the growing powers of the EP, which are not apparent to the everyday citizen.

All this boils down to a simple but powerful argument: if the EU is not a (nation) state, it cannot be democratised as nation states have been (Dehousse 1995). Even if it were, the Union could never use majoritarian approaches like liberal democracy and expect to measure up to national political systems in terms of legitimacy as viewed through the lens of liberal democracy, because it would be much bigger, with less closely bound senses of identity and community, operating at a greater geographical distance from the average citizen, and with a far greater population, which facts would reduce the capacity of the individual to play a constructive part in the demos either directly or through representatives (Weiler et al. 1995). Moreover, given that the EU is a polycentric system in which different kinds of policy regime coexist, there is no a priori reason why it should be democratised according to the same pattern in each policy area. For example, in policy areas such as biotechnology it may or may not be appropriate for experts to play a leading role via comitology, but there is no guarantee that the judgement about the acceptability or otherwise of their involvement in that issue would translate entirely to, say, agriculture. This point is reinforced by the emerging practice of flexibility: majoritarian approaches to democracy in the EU ignore that it is a system increasingly characterised by opt-outs and different speeds, implying that the constitution and membership of the 'European public' will change according to policy area. A more sophisticated and differentiated approach to democracy is therefore required (Warleigh 2002a, 2002b).

In sum, the EU polity requires an approach to democratisation which recognises that it is insufficiently politicised to allow for majoritarian practices to be expanded. Rightly or wrongly, the Union is commonly perceived as a technocracy whose workings are hermetic and arcane, dealing with fundamentally dull issues of regulation (Dehousse 1995) rather than issues of the 'big picture' (or at least those issues of general interest which are deemed suitable for transnational governance by the public (Blondel et al. 1998). There is a massive deficit of interest in, let alone engagement with, the EU. The eradication of this deficit requires coaxing and education as well as the provision of opportunities and structures. In addition, the mere fact of removal of national competence in a given policy area by globalization or the single European market does not automatically mean that citizens would welcome EU activism to fill the resulting gap (Beetham and Lord 1998; Scharpf 1999). This reveals a further dilemma: although the EU can no longer rely entirely on drawing legitimacy via national governments it must reach out to the citizens while continuing to derive at least part of its legitimacy from its ability to serve the 'national interest' (Höreth 1999). It must be prepared for the fact that citizens may well be critical of it for reasons other than ignorance, such as exclusion from decision-making or critique of Union policy/strategy.

Thus, the EU's dilemma is, *pace* the Governance White Paper of 2001, how to replace the Community Method with a form of democratisation which is sensitive to the EU's multi-level nature and flexibility, while generating a sense that the Union is a useful enterprise supported by a meaningful, if not necessarily 'thick', sense of community and solidarity. This method of democratisation will have to be expressly political, in order to avoid repetition of the problems of integration-by-stealth. It will have to take the existing institutional arrangements as a given (albeit an arrangement in need of reform), accepting that structure is important but also that what is currently vital is an emphasis on agency (in order to rework those structures with significant bottom-up input). It will also have to be substantive, i.e. capable of lending engaged citizens the ability to affect policy outcomes. It will have to accept as a given the existence of different perspectives, and seek not to aggregate or eradicate them but rather to find a way of managing them and arriving at a consensus which is broadly acceptable to all. Thus, there is a strong requirement to provide the means of deeper political socialisation and a sense of stakeholding, of popular reimagination of the Union as a system in which citizens should, and can, play a part. In short, the Union needs a form of democracy which privileges cross-border communication and discourse in order to generate a greater sense of community and at least the basis for engagement with, and reform of, the Union political system. These needs can be met by the application of a deliberativist model of democracy, as set out in the final section of this chapter.

What is to be done? The application of critical deliberativism

Explaining critical deliberativism

Deliberativists hold that democracy is best understood as the influence of 'reflective preferences' on public policy decisions (Dryzek 2000: 2). In other words, what makes for the best kind of democracy is the ability of all those concerned by a public policy to be engaged in a process of deliberation about it, that is, to exchange their views, to try to understand other actors' needs and perspectives, and thereby to reach a mutually agreeable outcome. Actors cooperate because they coexist in a given political space; in order to make mutually acceptable rules from a starting point at which they hold different perspectives and at which there is no hegemon capable of dictating the course of events, they engage in a process of negotiation and construction of a common interest, on matters of both principle and particular policy. This should not be seen as a process of bargaining, whereby interests are aggregated and turned into a package deal; instead, it is a process of learning and adaptation, in which issues are treated separately (giving no potential for log-rolling), and in which actors are prepared to change their preferences and views in order to accommodate other points of view. It is, therefore, a process of mutual education as well as a mechanism of mutual control. Deliberativists accept that there may well be limits to this process, and that ultimately no common view or consensus may be reachable. However, for deliberativists this indicates that there should also be limits to policy making; in the absence of a supportive base, it is better to have no policy than an illegitimate one. So, deliberativism ultimately sees democracy as a participatory rather than a representative practice: the franchise should be seen not (merely) as the right to vote, but as the ability to participate effectively in the formation of public policy (Dryzek 2000: 29). Democratic governance is an ongoing process of deliberation, based on free debate between political equals, pluralism, and mutual recognition as equals (Cohen 1997). Deliberativists also favour input legitimacy over output legitimacy: what counts most is the ability to shape public policy, because given that capacity to influence, an acceptable policy outcome is highly likely. However, transparency is a vital requirement of deliberative democracy, given that those who have deliberated must be able to see whether and how the fruits of their deliberations have impacted upon public life (Cohen 1997).

At the level of the citizen, deliberativism holds promise because it does not assume the pre-existence of a sense of community. Instead, it offers a mechanism by which individuals can cooperate and thereby generate a deeper sense of mutual understanding and, eventually, solidarity. It supplies a rationale for this cooperation – the fact of being bound by public policies of the same system. It also supplies a means by which individuals can cooperate despite their differences – deliberation – because this mechanism both expects differences to exist and provides the means by which they can be managed most effectively, and possibly even removed, by a process of mutual learning and accommodation. Thus, deliberativism offers a mechanism by which a sense of community can be constructed from the bottom-up, rather than imposed from the top-down (Dryzek 2000; Eriksen 2000). It offers the means by which policies can be justified as the product of political equality (equal participation in deliberation processes). It also shows how legitimacy can be generated (through a process of inclusion in decision making), and how socialisation can occur at both popular level, through a process of active citizenship and social learning (Christiano 1997), and also at elite level, through a process of iterated contact and communication (Risse 2000).

As a model for democratising international/transnational governance in the EU, deliberativism has three further major assets.[14] It can serve as a way of making decisions within each policy regime (so, even if each regime is configured differently, they may all work according to the same principle); it can be a means by which policy regimes are created (through negotiation and mutual agreement to extend the EU's scope); and it can serve as a means of adapting policy regimes/styles according to perceived need. Majoritarian approaches could also do this in theory, at least within any given institution; but in a cautious and occasionally stagnant intergovernmental context shaped by significant differences in national preferences, and also often by resistance to the perceived need to 'sacrifice' national sovereignty, deliberativism offers the means by which the EU can build further authority through 'consent and voluntary compliance' (Dryzek 1990: 106–7). This is an asset which must not be underestimated, given that the EU has limited capacity to force member states to comply with EC law, the insufficiently-applied (and ECJ-constructed) principle of state liability notwithstanding, and that in the Council the tendency has been to avoid using even qualified majority voting as much as possible (Sherrington 2000). At the level of inter-institutional dialogue and policy making processes, deliberativism has much to offer, given the primacy of networks and informal politics in producing policy outcomes (Peterson 1994). For example, the growing culture of codecision between Council and EP (Shackleton 2000) is capable of further development along deliberative lines.

However, it must be recognised that deliberative democracy, like any theoretical model, is unlikely to be capable of direct application to the real world of EU politics and policy making without adaptation. Deliberation has its limitations, some of which are general, and others of which reflect the peculiarities of the EU context. Therefore, what is necessary is a *critical* deliberative approach, in which deliberation forms the core of a coherent framework but in which elements of adjudicative and representative democracy are also present.

A critical theory is one which, to use the traditions of the Frankfurt School, seeks to undertake four tasks.[15] First, the enlightenment of agents, i.e. their empowerment to discover their true interests. Second, the emancipation of agents, i.e. their liberation from (possibly self-imposed) beliefs and structures which are inappropriate to the task at hand. Third, the production of forms of knowledge. Fourth, the pursuit of 'reflective' rather than 'objective' conceptualisations – in other words, to seek not the kind of neutral 'laws' established in natural science but rather an ongoing process of theoretical adaptation through critique, as an acknowledgement that theory and object/process of study are intricately linked. Critical theories must examine not just society and its institutions but also the beliefs people have about themselves and their society (including the theory itself).

The form of deliberativism I put forward is a critical theory insofar as it seeks to correct the hegemony of the liberal democratic blueprint for EU reform by questioning its origins and suitability. It is also 'critical' in that it seeks to produce a more appropriate form of democratisation (the emancipatory function). However, perhaps its key claim to being 'critical' is its commitment to reflect upon its own suitability, accepting that the required form of deliberative democracy must both reflect the specific needs of the EU system and the limits to 'pure deliberation' which the latter imposes. Thus, 'critical deliberativism' is intended in this book as a situation-specific conceptual framework which is open to the use of ideas from other traditions where this is appropriate and conceptually coherent. In this respect, it is in keeping with the pioneering work of Habermas (see inter alia 1984, 1987, 1996, 2000), who can be credited with reinventing critical theory in a less materialistic and instrumental direction than in its early incarnation (Alexander 1991). However, the present approach is not strictly Habermasian, in that I agree with both Eriksen (2000) and Chambers (1996) that his work tends to be perhaps too open to ideas of liberal democracy. For Eriksen, Habermas ultimately privileges the right over the good, a classical liberal choice. For Chambers, Habermas places too great an emphasis on institutions, thereby underestimating the degree to which deliberative democracy is dependent upon the establishment of a participatory political culture from the bottom-up. Accordingly, on a spectrum ranging between liberal and deliberative forms of democracy, the present approach is slightly closer to the deliberative end than Habermas'.

Additionally, what I mean by critical deliberativism is different from Dryzek's (2000) project although it shares the same general perspective. Dryzek's critical approach to deliberativism – 'discursive democracy' – seeks to make it applicable by attention to 'established power structures, including those that operate beneath the constitutional surface of the liberal state' (Dryzek 2000: 3-4). I share this general approach, and Dryzek's recognition of virtue in other forms of democracy than the deliberative, but seek here to make deliberation operationalisable in the context of the EU, which is not, as we have seen, a liberal state, but rather is composed of them.

The viability of deliberation in the EU context is open to question. It is true that deliberativism envisages the creation of common interests and understanding, rather than assuming their existence as a starting point, and also that it is capable of harnessing diversity as an asset in democratic communication (Young 1997). However, it is also true that citizens cannot create a new Europeanised public sphere through deliberativist practices if they cannot understand each other, and thus we are confronted with the problem of the lack of a common language in Europe. At the elite level, this is infrequently a problem; most actors in EU decision-making speak English or French sufficiently well to work together, and those who do not can rely on translators, at least in public meetings. Business, professional and media elites may well speak English; thanks to the American influence, English (or at least some form of it) is quite widely spoken by young people. However, this does not equate to the existence of a *lingua franca* in which every EU citizen is sufficiently competent to discuss matters of public importance rather than order a beer.

There are two issues to consider. First, how can citizens currently deliberate with each other across national borders? Second, if member states agree that there should be a common language, how long would it be before it was sufficiently widespread, and would it in fact face rejection as perceived linguistic imperialism? The likely answers to both questions indicate that, at least in the short–medium term, representative democracy may be necessary to overcome the linguistic divide. Monoglot EU citizens may have to rely on others to express their concerns in the EU arena, after an exercise of public deliberation akin to that undertaken in France to inform the 'post-Nice' process of institutional reform. In addition, or as an alternative, it might be possible to move towards a subdivision of the EU into cultural-linguistic clusters for the process of public deliberation, in which citizens of countries with sufficient linguistic affinities to allow mutual comprehension work together, and then enter into deliberations with the other clusters via representatives (Kraus 2000). Contributions to deliberative process via the internet offer further potential here (although principally as a forum for discussion groups rather than a device for the one-off posting of messages/opinions). Whatever the ultimate utility of such devices, it is clear that for the time being public deliberation will have to be channelled across borders in some way other than purely citizen-citizen.

Lord and Beetham (2001) make a further important point here, namely that deliberativists may overlook the issue of output legitimacy Christiano 1997). This is because a well-known feature of European integration is its production of unintended consequences of policy decisions, which then have to be managed in some way (Pierson 1996). It is true that another process of deliberation on these consequences could be launched, but it is also likely that 'deliberation fatigue' would soon set in given the limits of time and energy of even the most committed citizen. In the event of deliberation failing to produce consensus, particular policy proposals may be allowed to fall. Should this happen frequently, however, citizens may question the validity of the system, even if they 'own' it entirely (Gaus 1997).

Moreover, although one of deliberativism's strengths is its ability to reconcile differences of principle rather than policy preference (Bellamy 1995; Cohen 1997; Rawls 1997), it may be that these issues are intractable even by deliberation because even 'sincere reasoners [may] ... find themselves in principled disagreements' (Gaus 1997: 231). If a decision is necessary – either to preserve the credibility of the system or because of the issue's intrinsic salience – some form of institutional arbitration may be necessary (Gaus 1997). This in turn requires popular acceptance of the need for an arbitration function in the knowledge that such decisions may have to be made on grounds of 'utilitarian considerations concerning the good of the collectivity' (Bellamy 1995: 157). However, it is better to have such a function exercised by an interplay between 'interlocking democratic institutions' than by a 'court of putative moral experts' (Bellamy and Castiglione 1996: 123), given that issues of fundamental importance should be decided on a political (and hence relatively organic) rather than legal (and hence relatively fixed) basis if they are to be seen as legitimate. Moreover, it is important not to exaggerate the importance of pan-systemic responses to issues of policy or principle in the multi-level context of European integration; given the principles of subsidiarity and flexibility, or at least their more thorough articulation, there is no a priori reason why in many cases different opinions about the suitability of a given issue cannot successfully coexist (Warleigh 2002a).

Furthermore, an element of representative democracy may be necessary in the EU in order to ensure adequate supervision of the executive (and ensure the viability of the system) in general terms, not just on particular decisions. With imagination such a representative assembly could even function on deliberative rather than majoritarian lines (Lord and Beetham 2001: 458). However, any such institution would truncate the scope of politics based on citizen participation: this step may be necessary, but would have to be accompanied by a deeper process of socialisation in order to avoid the EU's current legitimacy problems. We need to reconcile the normative attractiveness of deliberative democracy (community-building and legitimacy-generation) with the more instrumental requirements of public policy production and system oversight in a contested process of polity-formation (Christiano 1997; Elster 1997; Gaus 1997).

Applying critical deliberativism to the EU: functionalist democracy[16]

There are two levels on which critical deliberativism must be applied to the EU: the macro (issues of system design, and the Union's developmental trajectory), and the micro (issues of policy making and system change). At the macro level, it is necessary to replace the federation-by-stealth objective of the Community Method with a more properly functionalist view of an evolving Europolity characterised by a diversity of levels and policy regimes, and itself conceived not as a state-in-waiting but as part of an international system of joint governance. For example, the existence of NATO is not to be seen as a threat to the development of the common foreign and security policy, but rather as the means by which it can be achieved more effectively as part of a broader alliance. This step is necessary because there is otherwise no guarantee that deliberativist integration outcomes short of state-creation will be seen as legitimate by federalists. By the same token, it offers the opportunity to legitimise integration in the eyes of all but the most entrenched Eurosceptics, by removing the perceived threat to national identity and power as much as possible. In this sense, critical deliberativism adds to the functionalist canon by enhancing its belief in gradualism and giving it the means by which it can make its democratic credentials at levels other than inter-state relations clearer (by adding to it the acceptance and deliberation of difference at popular level).

At the micro level, it is necessary to develop a more participatory system which can in turn support the creation of a Europeanised civic society through active citizenship (Bellamy 2001), and so provide both the EU and the integration process with further legitimacy. This is turn must be grounded in an acceptance that conflicts of interests and values are bound to arise in the EU, and must be treated as issues to be resolved collectively rather than problems to be eradicated by reference to doctrinaire views of either national sovereignty or federalism (Joerges 1997). Consequently, this must be accompanied by the embracing of flexible integration; if national or popular requirements of the EU are genuinely different, there is no democratic justification for the creation of a uniform system, and not just multi-speed but à la carte models of integration will be necessary (Warleigh 2002a).

In this way the prescriptions of liberal democracy are inappropriate for the EU. The application of critical deliberativism requires an acknowledgement of the value of representative forms of democracy as a complement to participatory democracy, but it also requires us to think beyond the model of the state as both the desired outcome of the integration process and as a reference point against which we measure the democratic status of the EU. Such a step is bold and requires a degree of experimentation. However, these are exactly the best attributes of the integration process, and in the following chapters I demonstrate how strategies of democratic reform in the EU have failed largely as a result of an omission to remember this innovative quality.

NOTES

1 Jean Monnet is credited with the elaboration of the strategy for European integration which became known as the 'Community' or 'Monnet' method. Although he made none of the formal decisions leading to the creation of this system, as a key bureaucrat, political adviser and international negotiator he proposed the plan for the European Coal and Steel Community (ECSC) to the then-responsible French minister, Robert Schuman, who brokered an agreement between France, Germany and the USA that it should be realised. Monnet was then tasked with negotiating the actual ECSC Treaty on behalf of France. He became the first President of the ECSC High Authority, and continued to have an influential role in the negotiation of subsequent treaties of European integration (Dinan 1999, Ch. 1; Holland 1994, Ch. 1).

2 By 'functionalist' I mean the theories put forward by such thinkers as David Mitrany. I explicitly do not mean the 'neofunctionalist' theories of, for example, Haas, Lindberg and Scheingold, whose attempts to make a 'social scientific' theory of regional integration used and, in my view, distorted certain of Mitrany's ideas. The so-called 'neo-functionalism', with its emphasis an teleological technocracy, was the academic reflection of the very Community Method I here criticise (Harrison 1974).

3 Japan joined the OECD in 1964, by which time it had become a forum for consideration of matters of the international economy, and less central to European integration (Urwin 1992: 22).

4 Exceptions were Yugoslavia and Albania (Davies 1997: 1100–04).

5 This claim persisted despite the Sino-Soviet split, which provided communist states with a rival global leader.

6 For excellent guides to the UK's difficult relationship with the EU, see George (1994) and Young (1998).

7 The main functionalist thinker was David Mitrany, whose key works include *The Progress of International Government* (1933), *A Working Peace System* (1944, 2nd edn) and *The Functional Theory of Politics* (1975). For excellent secondary guides to and critiques of functionalism, see Pentland (1973, 1975) and Taylor (1975, 1978a, 1978b) as well as Rosamond (2000a) and Warleigh (2002b).

8 The date of publication of Hancock's work is disputed.

9 Bellamy (1993) and Held (1988) demonstrate that liberal democracy can be both 'instrumental' and 'intrinsic' (or 'protective') – that is, it can be seen by its proponents as either a necessary tool of governance which must thus be borne or as an essential feature of democracy. However, as Bellamy (1993: 28) also argues, 'liberals … have tended to see government as having the essentially negative purpose of preserving the openness of society rather than as pursuing positive courses of action': in other words, they have tended to be instrumental in their approach to democracy, rather than intrinsic.

10 For useful guides to liberal democracy and its impact on structures of governance in Europe, see Dyson (1980), Wintrop (1983), Held (1988, 1993).

11 Liberals do, of course, differ considerably about what this minimum level actually is, with social liberals urging a limited, but not a minimal state, because they seek state intervention to promote equal opportunity (see Bellamy 1993). Moreover, especially since the advent of liberal feminism, there has been a re-evaluation of whether a strict divide between the public and private spheres is either possible or desirable.

12 Some liberals would argue, of course, that only the free market can guarantee individual liberty, but that this does not mean the state has no role in promoting some kind of social justice. See Rawls (1971).

13 In this light it is intriguing to consider Bellamy and Castiglione's (2000a) plea for 'democratic liberalism' in the EU. This model places a republican view of freedom as civic achievement rather than inherent attribute into liberal democracy, focusing on deliberation as the means by which a living constitution is created for the polity by its citizens. This model has clear links with the 'critical deliberativism' advocated in the present book, although the latter seeks a clearer break with liberal democracy in order to facilitate the process of creative thinking about novel forms of democratic governance for the innovative EU polity.

14 In this paragraph, I adapt the work of Dryzek (1990: 92–3) to the EU context. See also Risse (2000) for a discussion of how 'arguing', as he terms deliberation, can be useful in international (rather than specifically EU) politics.

15 In this paragraph I borrow from Geuss (1981).

16 It should be clear that I mean functionalism in its international relations sense, not in its anthropological/natural science sense (the idea that all objects, beliefs and traditions have an inherent purpose or function which is integral to the success of the entire organism/society).

3

Reconfiguring Sovereignty: Subsidiarity and Flexibility

Sovereignty, subsidiarity and flexibility

One of the main problems in addressing the 'democratic deficit' is the issue of how to weigh up the claims of (national) autonomy against the needs and wishes of the new, EU-level collective. The concept of national sovereignty which lies at the heart of this issue is one which continues to attract much rhetoric, and much abuse. National politicians continue to claim they have 'defended' national sovereignty against rapacious 'Brussels', as demonstrated clearly by the spin doctoring of the Nice Treaty in more member states than just the UK. Whatever the truths and inadequacies of such claims, they point to a vital issue in European integration: how much national sovereignty should be given up – or, in more EU-friendly terminology, 'pooled' – in order to secure the advantages to the member states of the integration process? Should this sovereignty be transferred to the EU as a new collective undertaking, or retained by the member states and merely delegated by them to the EU? When the wishes of a particular national government or population are clearly outside the EU mainstream, which view should prevail, and why? These questions lie at the heart of the EU's democracy problem, and continue to exercise the imagination of both politicians and academics.

This should not be taken to mean that national sovereignty is an unchanging given. Indeed, as I make clear below, national sovereignty is a *concept rather than a fact* (Camilleri and Falk 1992), and one which has been deliberately reconfigured in the EU context. This rearticulation is revealed in many practices of European integration (such as QMV, or the principle of member state liability for non-compliance with EU policy/EC law). However, the transformation of national sovereignty in and by the EU is presented most clearly in the concepts of subsidiarity and flexibility, both of which speak explicitly to the relationship between the member states and the EU as a collective, and both of which explicitly address the twin issues of where power should lie in the EU, and how that power should be exercised. Although both subsidiarity and flexibility have roots much earlier in the integration process, they rose to prominence by framing the debates about the Union throughout the 1990s. In the early part of the decade, the pre- and post-Maastricht debates on designing the integration process centred on subsidiarity; by the latter end of the decade, flexibility had become the in-vogue term, a status it still maintains. Thus, national sovereignty and its reconfiguration continue to inform current debates on EU reform.

In this chapter I argue that subsidiarity and flexibility have much in common as means by which national sovereignty has been reconfigured with some success in the EU.[1] I also argue that the continuing weaknesses in Treaty elaboration, and inadequacies in EU governance practice, of both these concepts has severely truncated their ability so far to help remedy the democratic deficit. Both concepts remain controversial; moreover, and more tellingly, they also remain ambiguous and under-determined. However, with sufficient elaboration, these twin concepts could contribute much to the democratic renewal of EU governance.

The structure of the chapter is as follows. In the next section, I explore the concept of sovereignty, and set out an understanding of what it means in the contemporary EU context. Subsequently I examine the concept of subsidiarity, and detail its contribution to the debate on EU democracy. I then treat the concept of flexibility similarly. Finally, I conclude that subsidiarity and flexibility share common problems of inadequate articulation and implementation, and have thus been able to make only a limited contribution to the resolution of the EU's democracy problem.

Sovereignty: the Gordian knot of integration

Sovereignty is a concept which owes its existence to the European tradition of the state, which began in the late middle ages (Treaty of Westphalia 1648) and reached a more contemporary incarnation in the wake of the French Revolution of 1789. As political organisation moved beyond feudalism towards state-building and the centralization of political authority, the doctrine of sovereignty was invented as a means to underpin and advocate this large socio-political change (Camilleri and Falk 1992; Curtin 1997). Thinkers such as Bodin and Hobbes developed the concept of sovereignty as the legitimiser of exclusive control of a given territory by a central authority, linking it to related ideas such as the national interest, independence and security. This is the idea of *national (or state) sovereignty*.

Thinkers such as Kant and Rousseau argued differently, i.e. that sovereignty is the concept by which public power is legitimised as the expression of the popular will. This is the concept of *popular sovereignty*. A central debate in political theory ever since has been on the best way to express and combine these two concepts, with the idea of the liberal democratic nation state often considered the optimum marriage of the two (Newman 1996; see also Chapter 1). In terms of European integration, it has generally been national sovereignty which is considered in need of defence or rearticulation, although the two kinds of sovereignty are often confused.[2]

In short, the formation of new and powerful means of governing a territory required both justification to those bound by it, and agreement by actors outside its scope not to interfere. Thus, the idea of (state) sovereignty was elaborated as the means by which the state could be legitimised as the defender of a given group of people against potential aggressors, and as the principle according to which that group of people had a normative right to their independence from other groups. State sovereignty is a set of rules according to which different states recognise each other as equals, claiming the monopoly of power within their own borders in return for a recognition of other actors' equivalent monopoly over a different territory. In the words of Camilleri and Falk, sovereignty is a means 'not only to describe political and economic arrangements but to explain and justify them as if they belonged to the natural order of things' (1992: 11). For Curtin, '(t)he principle of state sovereignty did not appear out of thin air. It embodies a historically specific account of ethical possibility in the form of an answer to questions about the nature and location of political community' (1997: 12).

Krasner (1999) has elaborated a very useful four-fold typology of sovereignty which is invoked in Figure 3.1 to add further clarity to the above discussion.

TYPE OF SOVEREIGNTY	MEANING
International legal sovereignty	Mutual recognition of independence by different states
Westphalian sovereignty	Exclusion of external actors ('foreigners') from authority within a state
Domestic sovereignty	Formal organisation of political authority within a territory
Interdependence sovereignty	Ability to regulate all cross-border flows

Source: adapted from Krasner 1999: 3–4

FIGURE 3.1   KRASNER'S TYPOLOGY OF SOVEREIGNTY

For Krasner, these four variants of sovereignty coexist: although loss or compromise of one variant does not entail the total loss of sovereignty, in order to be fully sovereign a state must have the monopoly of all of them. Thus, very few states in history have actually been fully sovereign. Moreover, in particular Westphalian and international legal sovereignties have been subject to massive violation throughout history, as actors in suitably powerful positions have ignored the claims to sovereignty of other actors by means both crude (invasion) and more subtle (e.g. the imposition of conditions upon a state's recognition as legitimate by other actors, such as putting in place a suitable human rights regime, or obeying the diktats of international financial organisations such as the IMF). Thus, as in the sub-title of Krasner's book, sovereignty is ultimately a kind of 'organised hypocrisy': it is routinely presented as the ultimate political value, but is in fact a principle honoured as much in the breach as in the practice, often with good reason (e.g. the imposition of sanctions on South Africa under the apartheid regime).

The above definitions of sovereignty shed light on the two principal – and somewhat contradictory – reasons why it has been such a controversial principle in European integration. First (national) sovereignty is part of what might be considered the European political tradition, with deep roots in the theories and practices of the state. Thus, its existence appears 'natural' to citizens. Furthermore, it means that those honestly seeking to present a 'European political identity' must acknowledge that, rightly or wrongly, and the followers of Kant notwithstanding, in terms of relations between states and their respective publics this identity has usually centred on difference and independence, not similarity and interdependence. Second, European integration cruelly exposes the hollowness of orthodox views of sovereignty by demonstrating time and again that the member states are in fact deeply interdependent.

Practice and rhetoric are completely out of kilter; moreover, rhetoric about preserving (state) sovereignty in the EU context adds to the perception of the democratic deficit because it both entrenches a bunker mentality and is of increasingly evident mendacity. This is particularly problematic in member states such as the UK where Euroscepticism is strong, because those who are opposed to the EU cannot rightly be gainsaid when they allege it weakens (although it does not entirely remove) UK sovereignty through the supremacy of EC law, QMV, state liability for non-compliance etc. In a context where sovereignty is seen as a zero-sum treasure to be 'defended' or 'preserved', its loss or alteration cannot be justified, only denied. The case for European integration, worthy though it is, is therefore rendered very difficult to make; sovereignty is in this regard the Gordian knot of European integration, whose untangling (or cutting, in swashbuckling Alexandrian fashion) is impossible without an ideological leap.

This great shift is necessitated by the fact that accession to the Union has altered the member states' sovereignty in both practical and conceptual terms, because it has removed 'the congruence between territory, identity and function which characterised the nation state' (Laffan 1998: 238). This is a consequence of the depth and breadth of the European integration project; other international organisations do not have the same reach in terms of policy scope, or strength, as represented by the relative autonomy and power of the EU institutions and the (challenged) supremacy of EC law (Laffan 1998). There are real-world shifts in the practice of sovereignty by EU member states which practitioners are usually reluctant publicly to admit, even when they are fully aware of them.[3] Indeed, for Krasner (1999: 228–37), the EU can even be considered an *alternative* to sovereignty, a body politic with extensive territory, recognition by external actors, authority beyond its own borders and significant supranational power, but yet also deep roots in the member states, which use the Union as a means of exercising and truncating their sovereignty.

Similar views of plural sovereignty are shared by many commentators, who point out that sovereignty (understood as autonomy and ability to influence agendas or outcomes) is partially wielded by several institutions and groups within the multi-level and complex EU system (e.g. Bellamy and Castiglione 1997). Thus, in the EU context, sovereignty is correctly considered to be not only a matter of relative state power, but also one of popular participation in, and control over, Union decision making (returning to the debate between state and popular sovereignties). The democratic deficit lies, in this reading, in the under-development of popular sovereignty at EU level. This set of ideas is perhaps demonstrated most clearly by MacCormick (1999).

For MacCormick, the problem of sovereignty in the EU is exemplified in the debate over *kompetenz-kompetenz* (the ability to determine who has the ability to define limits to legitimate political or legal authority) in the wake of the Maastricht Treaty. This issue was raised most notoriously by the *Brunner* case, in which the ratification of the Maastricht Treaty by Germany was challenged ([1994] 1 Common Market Law Reports 57). To simplify considerably, the German Constitutional Court (Bundesverfassungsgericht, BVerfG) ruled, in essence, that the Treaty did not pose a challenge to the democratic values of the German state, and could thus be ratified. However, the BverfG stated that it considered European integration could eventually reach such a point, and that it reserved the right to determine, in the name of the German people, when that point had been reached, and to reject any Treaty it considered illegitimate on these grounds.[4]

In terms of the politics of EC law, this boils down to a dispute over which body has the authoritative voice in determining the legitimate scope of EU policy and activity: the European Court of Justice (ECJ), or the constitutional/highest courts of the member states? The ECJ has claimed that it holds this power as a result of its own decision that the EU Treaties have a 'constitutional' character, and the similarly ECJ-established principle of the supremacy of EC law (the concept that if EC law and member state law are in conflict, EC law must be adhered to). Courts at the apex of national systems have often held that EC law is binding only insofar as domestic constitutional law permits this; in other words, their view is that the supremacy of EC law is partial and delegated, and thus ultimately revocable if it challenges principles which are vital within member state legal/constitutional traditions. Thus, although on a day-to-day basis the lower national courts and the ECJ have collaborated to build a solid EC legal order (Hunt 2001), the *kompetenz-kompetenz* issue is far from settled.

For MacCormick (1999: 142), this means that neither the EU nor the individual member states can accurately be considered 'sovereign' in traditional terms. Instead, the EU is a 'post-sovereign' entity described as a 'European Commonwealth' and composed of 'no longer absolutely sovereign states interacting with and through a Community with an independent legal order of its own'. The functions and tasks traditionally ascribed to the state remain, but some of them have been redistributed to different governance actors, including those at EU level. In practice, sovereignty is being rearticulated and contested, rather than forgotten or transcended, even if public rhetoric often fails to express this. It is therefore useful to examine subsidiarity and flexibility as crucial indicators of how successful this process of reconfiguring sovereignty has been.

Subsidiarity: ambiguity and incompleteness

Subsidiarity is an interesting example of how concepts can be used to mean anything, and hence nothing at all, in the context of European integration. Those seeking to defend the EU, and its potential democratic credentials in particular, have located the principle as the heart of European democratic thought which the EU can now take forward to its conclusion in a federal *finalité politique* (Pinder 1991; Vignon 1993). Those seeking to defend national autonomy have hailed the principle as the ultimate expression of that notion (see the discussion in Peterson 1994). This does not mean that subsidiarity is a useless concept; it does mean that its current form in the Treaty is ambiguous and incompletely articulated. In this section of the chapter I explore several related issues, which I separate out for clarity while acknowledging their interdependence. First, the issue of defining subsidiarity (which has been a great cause of contestation). Second, the issue of clarifying the link between subsidiarity and its close cousin, proportionality.

Third, the contribution which subsidiarity could make to the reduction of the democratic deficit in theory, and the somewhat less impressive impact that it has been able to make in practice.

For many commentators, subsidiarity is the essence of federalism in that it is a concept dealing with the relations between different tiers of power and also between the individual and the group/the state (Vignon 1993). Thus, the principle can be traced back to classical political thinkers such as Aristotle (Höffe 1996). In fact, as pointed out by Peterson (1994: 117–9) there are three main roots of subsidiarity as applied to the EU. First, there is Catholic (and later, Christian Democrat) social philosophy, which argues that power should be exercised by organisations and groups at the lowest possible level, and that social groups, rather than the state per se, should be empowered. Second, there is the German federal/legalistic tradition, which requires a clear separation of powers between the EU and the member states (and their regions), as well as a clear constitution and outcome of the integration process. Third, there is the UK government view,[5] which argues that subsidiarity is the principle according to which the powers of the EU must be limited, and those of the member states preserved.

Although there are common threads here – notably the ideas that power should be held at the lowest possible level, and that an omnipotent central authority at the EU level is to be avoided – there are also clear differences. Catholic social philosophy places great importance on civil society; German federalism emphasises a strong (albeit decentralised) state structure, and the UK reading of the principle emphasises national autonomy in highly communitarian fashion. Thus, there is no agreement about what the 'lowest possible level' actually is. Nor is there a common view of what kind of structure should be developed at EU level, or the balance of power between it, the member states, the regions, and civil society.

Moreover, the Treaty refers to subsidiarity in two very different ways. The first is as a substantive principle, according to which decisions must be taken as closely to the citizen as possible. The second is as a procedural criterion, to be used to decide how and when the EU should act (Scott et al. 1994). This reflects both the different understandings of the principle outlined immediately above and the reasons why it was included in the Maastricht Treaty.

Although references to subsidiarity had been made in EU circles since at least the Tindemans report of 1975, and mention of it was made in the SEA (1986), it is only with the Treaty on European Union that any attempt was made to elaborate it as a principle capable of explicitly informing EU governance (Green 1994; Scott et al. 1994). Even then it was essentially a principle of second choice, to which recourse was made only because the UK government refused to accept a reference to the EU's 'federal vocation' in the Treaty (Peterson 1994). The form given to subsidiarity in the Treaty was the result of a typical EU package deal, in which no clear vision was present but in which actors defending all three understandings of the principle could claim to see evidence that their view was taken into account (Green 1994).

Given the context of the Maastricht negotiations, and the subsequent difficult ratification of that Treaty, subsidiarity achieved greater prominence as a means of placating actors concerned about a federal outcome to the integration process in the UK Parliament, and in the Danish public (Peterson 1994). Thus, a principle supposed to be either the essence of, or a substitute for, federalism, was publicly used as its antithesis not just by Eurosceptic governments, but by the European Council, in an attempt to persuade the Danes to reverse their rejection of the Treaty. Moreover, the possibility of reading subsidiarity as a principle which could allow a greater voice for the citizen, or civil society, was removed. The Edinburgh Declaration on subsidiarity, made at the European Council summit in Edinburgh of December 1992, effectively narrowed the principle down to the point that it became a loose means of regulating the balance of power between the EU and the member states. The latter imposed three strict criteria for the elaboration of policy by the EU. First, the Commission has to demonstrate that it has a suitable legal base in the Treaty for what it is proposing (effectively ruling out the use of the Treaty provisions on adding to the EU's remit without an IGC, if this is necessary to secure an agreed policy goal). Second, the Commission has to show that action at the national and/or regional level is insufficient to secure the policy objective. Third, all EU activity must be kept to the minimum necessary (Peterson 1994). Of course, these criteria are capable of different interpretations. However, they do indicate that the UK Tory view ultimately prevailed over its competitors in the interpretation of subsidiarity, at least in the post-Maastricht period. Subsequent Treaty reforms at Amsterdam and Nice have done little to reverse this; the Amsterdam Treaty provided a new Protocol on Subsidiarity, which slightly increased its clarity but continued the trend towards using subsidiarity as a procedural device rather than a normative principle (de Búrca 1998; Follesdal 2000). The Nice Treaty left such issues untouched, although they form part of the debates of the Convention set up to inform the next IGC.

In this light, it is not surprising that there are clear limits to the present utility of subsidiarity as a tool of EU governance, let alone a principle by which the democratic deficit could meaningfully be addressed. Perhaps some of these limitations were inevitable; if we understand the Union as an evolving and unusual system of governance, it would be a mistake to expect a clear and irrevocable separation of powers at this stage of its development (Laffan et al. 2000). However, other shortcomings are less justifiable. For example, the ambiguity of subsidiarity means that the role of the ECJ in interpreting the Treaty provisions may well be great, and yet there are clear normative reasons why such a role should be avoided on the grounds that such decisions are political, not judicial (Emiliou 1992). This issue of the justiciability of subsidiarity is highly nuanced: the balance between legal and political judgement is very easy to upset, and the Court could face many problems if it ruled controversially or were seen to allow challenges to either national or EC law on the grounds of subsidiarity (Emiliou 1992). And yet, it is impossible to rule out any role for the ECJ in such matters, even if this role is played out cautiously; indeed, some commentators (Duff 1997) heralded the Protocol on Subsidiarity of the Amsterdam Treaty on the grounds that it clarified the justiciability of the principle.

The issue of justiciability is compounded by the conceptual ambiguities of subsidiarity. Höffe (1996) points out that subsidiarity and democracy can be in conflict with each other. If legitimately elected public actors pass laws which do not serve the individual or allow their autonomy, they may be 'democratic', but they will not reflect the principle of subsidiarity, at least insofar as Catholic social theory understands it. For some commentators, subsidiarity is therefore a *social* principle rather than one capable of informing politico-legal constitutional questions (Höffe 1996);[6] thus, EU actors attempting to use it in this way are using an inappropriate tool. Certainly, it has failed to be capable of use as a means of improving the position of regional governments within the EU system. The German Länder, so crucial in brokering the Treaty compromise wording in alliance with the UK government (Green 1994), did not achieve their goal of using it to usher in a 'Europe of the Regions', and instead have pursued their primary interests by other means (Jeffery 2000). This is because the Treaty explicitly limits subsidiarity to EU-member state relations (Follesdal 2000; Scott et al. 1994). Thus, subsidiarity has not served to allow those governance actors at the level closest to the citizen – local/regional governments – to play a greater role in the integration process, a gap which has not yet been made good by the creation of the legislatively weak, if sometimes influential, Committee of the Regions (Warleigh 2001e).

The concept of proportionality is another useful issue for consideration here. As mentioned above, the Edinburgh Declaration on subsidiarity made clear that it would be used as a means to ensure that the EU's role as a legislator was restricted. This indicates that subsidiarity as articulated in the EU is almost reducible to proportionality – the principle that action should only be taken by the Union when absolutely vital, and to the minimum extent necessary to achieve the goal. Although the two principles are closely related (perhaps particularly in the Catholic social theory of the state, and in the UK Conservative view of EU action), there is a key issue here because proportionality is predominantly managerial in nature, whereas subsidiarity is more explicitly normative. Subsidiarity, on the one hand, determines who should act, and when. (It appears that the normative choice here has been to restrict the capacity of the EU to act.) Proportionality, on the other hand, follows on from this normative choice to dictate that one particular set of actors – those at the EU level – should adopt a minimalist policy style. Thus, subsidiarity has not been used to foster debate about the big political issues of European integration – who should do what, why, and when – but instead has been used as a misguiding label to justify a default position that the EU should act as little as possible, even if this implies a loss of efficiency or welfare.

It follows from this that subsidiarity has a very limited utility in the bid to rectify the democratic deficit, at least in its current variant. Beetham and Lord (1998) argue that in theory subsidiarity means the EU can no longer rely on indirect legitimacy via its member states. This is because subsidiarity implies that the Union should concern itself only with issues which are beyond the scope of individual action by the member states, and are thus supranational by definition. And yet, the primacy of proportionality over subsidiarity in the decade since Maastricht has meant that this is precisely the kind of logic that the principle is incapable of reflecting. In a generous reading of the Amsterdam Protocol on subsidiarity, Follesdal (2000) argues that the Protocol does make centralisation of power more difficult by elaborating a 'relative efficiency' test, and this can be read as a democratic defence against tyranny. However, Follesdal also notes that this very test, added to national governments' continued refusal to extend the subsidiarity principle below the level of the member state, removes much of subsidiarity's democratic potential because it gives centrality to managerial issues rather than those of principle, and fails to address the fact that the member states are 'institutionally entrenched in ways difficult to justify by any theory of subsidiarity' (Follesdal 2000: 106–7).

A final difficulty of the relationship between democracy and subsidiarity is that of the non-existent link between the concept of subsidiarity and public views of what the EU should do. No attempt has so far been made to match the competences of the EU to public opinion on what is appropriate competence for the Union (Blondel et al. 1998; Sinnott 1994), or even to change that opinion in order to reflect the EU's current competences by means of an extensive debate. Thus, a central feature of an important theory of subsidiarity – the Catholic social variant – is ignored, and the individual remains on the periphery of EU decision making. Moreover, the policy competences of the EU remain the result of accumulated package deals and institutional entrepreneurship, an elite choice rather than that of the general public(s). It remains to be seen whether the post-Laeken convention and the process of 'civil dialogue' can rectify this situation, and thereby restore some legitimacy to the use of the term 'subsidiarity' to describe a key principle of EU governance.

Flexibility: the reluctant norm of EU governance

By contrast, flexibility has seemingly travelled from being an unspecified if frequent *practice* of EU governance to the point where it is being slowly (and so far, inadequately) fleshed out as a leading *principle* of democratic governance in the EU. A concept with a long EU history, flexibility has the potential to aid the reconfiguration of national sovereignty by both justifying its continued 'sacrifice' or 'pooling' at EU level, and by making that process subject to clear limits set on an iterative basis according to explicit political choice (Warleigh 2002a). However, the member states have so far been unable to move beyond recourse to flexibility as a useful but ad hoc means of reconciling differences between them and towards setting out in a clear way exactly how it could guide EU governance. This is because such a choice involves facing difficult questions about the future of the EU and what each member state wants from it. In this section of the chapter I define flexibility, and set out its potential as well as the barriers to its articulation as such a principle of democratic EU governance. I argue that the principal impediments to the realisation of this goal are the continuing centrality of the federal frame in determining the views of the desirable end product of integration held by many of those who advocate a more democratic EU, and resistance to real flexibility by governments who seek to use it as a cloak for Euroscepticism.

Flexibility has gained ascendancy for the principal reason that it is a tool for the management of diversity. The member states continue to want different things from, and outcomes of, the integration process; flexibility builds on the lead of QMV (which of course obliges all member states to participate in generally agreed policy, whether they supported it or not) to ensure that recalcitrant states cannot always dictate the pace to the others (Gillespie 1997). This has enabled many of the most successful and ambitious recent EU measures to be realised (EMU, the creation of the Rapid Reaction Force (RRF)). At the level of individual policies, flexibility has also proved valuable by reconciling the different goals of the various states (Bailey 1999). Thus, at both macro and micro levels, flexibility is a means by which member states can agree new policies despite the continuing existence of often important differences between them, constituting 'a way to find compromise and avoid logjam' (Stubb 1997: 47). As a result, at least in theory[7] flexibility can delegitimise collective action by member states outside the EU structures in areas of EU competence, at least if the intention behind such action is to remain outside these structures (Dewatripont et al. 1995). This is because if reluctant member states are allowed to opt out of a policy measure, while member states which share objectives are allowed to pursue them as EU policy, there is little justification for other kinds of multi-lateral action on that issue by those member states. Flexibility also has potential to help reduce the democratic deficit, because it is underpinned by a high respect for difference, and thus for managing, but also respecting, diversity (Warleigh 2002b).

Flexibility is controversial, however, because it can be read as inter-governmentalism, i.e. as an attempt by the member states to slow down the process of integration. For some scholars, flexibility is simply a part of the process by which the member states sought to exert a greater control over the EU and its institutions during the 1990s (Devuyst 1999; Moravcsik and Nicolaidis 1999). Others have argued that flexibility is a substitute for addressing the real issues of importance on the EU agenda, by avoiding dis-cussion of the common *finalité politique* (Chaltiel 1998). Still others have argued that flexibility is in fact most likely to be the product of the attempt by key member states (such as France and Germany) to establish themselves at the heart of the EU, and thus control its agenda ever more tightly to the detriment of those opposed to their preferences. Monnet (1978) con-sidered that flexibility was evidence of an integration process gone awry, because it represented the failure of the EU institutions to eclipse the authority of their national equivalents, and the failure of inter-state soli-darity to vanquish the differences between them. Neofunctionalists such as Haas (1975) shared this view. As a result, proponents of flexibility are obliged to assuage the concerns of many actors at both EU and national level and show that it can deepen (or at least not impede) the integration process. This advocacy is difficult because it calls into question the ortho-dox views of what the integration process should achieve, in the view of those most strongly attached to it. It is made even more problematic by the confusion about what flexibility actually means; even more than in the case of subsidiarity there is great confusion about the term flexibility, leading one leading commentator to refer to the plethora of understandings and counter-readings as a case of 'semantic indigestion' (Stubb 1996). Indeed, it should also be recognised that member states seeking to prevent further deepening have often been reluctant to allow the clearer articulation of flexi-bility in order to retain their ability to veto step changes in the integration process (Taylor 1996), a fact to which can be attributed much of the EU's relative stagnation in the 1970s (Taylor 1983).

Before taking the present analysis much further, then, it is helpful to provide a typology of flexibility in order to approach a working definition. In order to do this I set out three models of flexibility. However, it must be remembered that the Treaty provisions on flexibility – or 'closer coopera-tion' as it is somewhat coyly dubbed – simultaneously evince aspects of all three models (Warleigh 2002a, Chapter 1). Moreover, flexibility works differently in each pillar of the EU. In pillar 1, the Commission has a de facto veto right in that it must approve all proposed closer cooperation measures. If co-decision applies to legislation produced through closer cooperation,

Model	Main Cause of Differentiation	Vision of Integration
Multi-speed	Inability to implement policy (short term)	Policy regimes with different members, laggards commit to catch up over time
Concentric circles	Inability to implement policy (long term)	Various tiers of member states around a hard core
À la carte	Choice not to participate in certain policies	Policy regimes with different memberships over the long term

Source: Warleigh 2002a

FIGURE 3.2   MODELS OF FLEXIBILITY

the EP has a similar power, as it must approve such proposals by the assent procedure (i.e. it can approve or disapprove, but not amend, the proposal). The scope for flexibility is narrow in pillar 2, and all power is with the Council of Ministers (using QMV). In pillar 3, the procedure is similar, but the scope is somewhat wider.

The typology shown in Figure 3.2 of flexibility distinguishes between the models according to two main variables: the degree of differentiation they envisage and the period of time for which this differentiation is considered acceptable.

Multi-speed integration is essentially a means to conceptualise what is a common historical feature of European integration, i.e. the initial implementation of policies by those member states immediately capable of so doing, and the subsequent implementation of the relevant policies by those member states without the initial capacity as soon as they have it. In this model, the main variable is thus capacity, not divergence of policy interest or principle; all member states agree that they will eventually adopt the same policies. This model tends to be solidaristic, in that those member states which launch the policy have a duty to help their colleagues catch up (Tindemans 1976). Thus, differentiation between the member states is considered a temporary and unfortunate necessity. An example is the numerous derogations from EU policy granted to many member states throughout Union history.

The *concentric circles* model, however, assumes that certain member states are incapable of adopting certain policies for long periods of time, if not for ever. It advocates that the EU should thus be reorganised into divisions rather like a football league: Union policy should be divided into discrete sections, and each member state should then join the division which reflects its capacities (or perhaps will, although the emphasis is on capacity) to implement the legislation. An example is the plan for a 'hard core' of member states composed of France, Germany and Benelux (Lamers 1997). Promotion into a higher 'division' is possible if a member state makes the necessary improvements in capacity. Nonetheless, this model at base expects and advocates more-or-less permanent differentiation between the member states across a range of policy areas rather than in individual sections of the *acquis*. This model has been applied to the EU more often in theory than in practice; there is as yet no single group of member countries which constitute a clear laggard group (although both the UK and Denmark are outside both the Schengen legislation and the single currency, they are joined by Ireland in the first case, and Sweden in the second).

À la carte versions of flexibility reflect the first two models, although there is a very important new variable to consider here. Both multi-speed and concentric circle models take capacity to implement EU policy as the primary reason for differentiation between member states; à la carte models are predicated on *political will*, i.e. a deliberate decision not to participate. As in multi-speed models, à la carte approaches advocate a pattern of core-periphery relations which differs according to the policy issue, and not a formal separation of the EU into different and essentially permanent tiers of membership. However, like concentric circles models, à la carte approaches are prepared to accept such patterns of differentiation as enduring, although at any time a non-participant member state could change its mind. Although the EU does not generally use this model, it has been adopted on occasion, as exemplified by the UK opt-out from much social policy (subsequently rejected on the election of the Labour government of 1997).

Although the Maastricht Treaty allowed flexibility to be used in order to implement 'history-making' (Peterson 1995) policy such as the single currency, it was only with the Amsterdam and Nice Treaties that flexibility was articulated with any clarity as a feature of EU governance. As always in the EU, flexibility has evolved over time instead of emerging as a fully-fledged principle in a 'big bang'. However, its articulation in the Treaty remains unclear, and cautious. This is because the choice between flexibility as a device of polity management and a principle of EU governance has yet to be made (Shaw 1998; Warleigh 2002b), although the pressures of enlargement to Central and Eastern European countries have caused the member states to articulate flexibility more clearly than in the past (Philippart 2001).

The Treaty of Amsterdam established that member states could opt out not only from whole policy areas, but also from individual measures within that policy field – even if they adopted all or most related measures. For example, in pillar 2 the notion of 'constructive abstention' was established. This means that a member state opposed to a proposal can abstain rather than veto, and thus allow the proposal to go ahead. Other types of flexibility were established for pillars 1 and 3. In pillar 1, the Commission was given a de facto veto power over the use of closer cooperation, but in pillars 2 and 3 the Council retained almost all power over its use. In all pillars member states opposed to the use of closer cooperation to make policy were given the right to prevent its invocation, although the use of the veto was subject to appeal by other member states in the European Council. In pillar 1, the European Parliament and ECJ were empowered in decision-making under closer cooperation exactly as under 'normal' decision-making, although they would have no ability to invoke or block the use of closer cooperation itself (Kortenberg 1998). Policies made under closer cooperation would be paid for by those member states which took part, not from the EU budget per se.

However, the Amsterdam Treaty left many questions about flexibility unanswered. First, closer cooperation had a very clumsy triggering mechanism, in which multiple vetoes existed, making it unclear whether closer cooperation measures were in fact capable of launch (Ehlermann 1998). Second, closer cooperation was placed within strict limits, such as the injunction not to undermine EU citizenship, and the fact it was to be used as a last resort. Furthermore, it could not be used to add to the EU's set of competences, only to make policy under existing competences. Third, the scope of its application remained unclear (Shaw 1998). Fourth, it was unclear how many member states would constitute a quorum for closer cooperation measures (Kortenberg 1998). Thus, closer cooperation as in the Amsterdam Treaty was unable to allow member states seeking to deepen EU competence to do so (Philippart and Edwards 1999; Scharpf 1999); it did not, as a result, provide sufficient reason for member states seeking to collaborate to do so within, rather than outside, the EU framework.

These issues were addressed, to some extent, by the Nice Treaty. The national veto on the launch of closer cooperation was abolished; the EP was given the ability to veto the launch of closer cooperation if it would have codecision rights under subsequent legislation (which means the triggering mechanism is still clumsy, but which at least reduces fears that the EP might be sidelined by closer cooperation); in pillar 3, the Commission was empowered roughly as in pillar 1, and decisions in Council about whether a member state can join the vanguard group can now be made by QMV; the quorum for closer cooperation measures is set at eight member states (the specific number, rather than the requirement of a majority of member states, is in the Treaty); and the meaning of 'last resort' is slightly clarified by the introduction of a relative efficiency criterion. Thus, the key criterion in judging whether or not closer cooperation measures can be launched is whether they would enable the EU to meet its objectives (or at least those of 8 member states) more successfully and more rapidly than action by the entire EU (Warleigh 2002a). This is an intriguing parallel with subsidiarity's translation into proportionality, as described above.

However, these significant changes were made in order to make flexibility a potentially helpful tool of polity management rather than in order to articulate it as a clear principle of Union governance. As Gillespie (2001) demonstrates, although certain of the restrictions on the use of closer cooperation are removed by the Nice Treaty, others are put in their place. Flexibility still cannot be used to add to the EU's set of competences; moreover, like subsidiarity, it does not apply to areas of exclusive EU competence. Flexibility is ruled out in certain areas where it might potentially be of great utility, e.g. much of pillar 2 (matters with defence or military implications). There is a notable injunction to respect 'economic and social cohesion', which, while capable of lax interpretation, constitutes a clear potential barrier to the emergence of vanguard groups in many policy areas. Thus, flexibility requires much further elaboration if it is to be optimally useful.

However, such elaboration will have to confront several significant problems (Warleigh 2002a, Chapter 4). If it is insufficiently translated into Treaty provisions and governance practices, flexibility might simply make the EU less transparent and more complex, without any attendant benefits of deepening or legitimacy. The relationship between member states participating in any closer cooperation regime and the non-participants, and also the relationship between the participant states and the EU institutions, remain to be clarified, even if there is an unwritten understanding that only in the Council will nationals from non-participant member states have no role in decision-making (Neunreither 2000a). It remains unclear whether political choice, or technical incapacity, should be the primary or exclusive reason for opting out. Thus, there has yet to be a clear choice between the different models of flexibility, which makes the provisions on closer cooperation a somewhat uneasy and ambiguous compromise. The relationship between the EU and other parts of the European 'condominio' (Schmitter 1996b) remain to be clarified: is the EU to be one cooperative regime among many, or the heart of the continental governance system – and will this choice vary according to policy area? Is flexibility to be an alternative to, or part of, the shift away from the traditional Community Method? Can, and should, flexibility be restricted to certain policy areas, and if so, which ones? Would flexibility undermine the EU's ability to act effectively on the world stage, or undermine EC law? If unleashing flexibility either creates or permits inequalities, would this make the EU less democratic?

Such problems are capable of solution, but they require critical re-examination of orthodox approaches to European integration. Flexibility is not a panacea for the problems of EU governance, but its contribution to their resolution will only be made if it is fully deployed, and this calls for the abandonment of the notion that integration is a process leading to a European federal state – at least, insofar as the totality of the member states are concerned. (Flexibility is perfectly commensurable with the federation of a sub-group of member states.) In turn, this requires a conceptual leap from the view that flexibility is a tool of polity management to be brought out of the box when all else has failed, to the view that flexibility should be a, or possibly the, *leitmotif* of the integration process (Warleigh 2002a, 2002b). Clearly, such would be a significant reorientation of the Union, both normatively and practically. From the point of view of democratic theory, it points towards a progressive, deliberative approach, rather than one derived from liberal democracy. However, without such a step-change, flexibility is likely to repeat the fate of subsidiarity, and constitute a potentially useful, but under-developed, idea which is sacrificed on the altar of member state refusal to be open about the consequences of European integration for national sovereignty.

Conclusions: the difficulties of reconfiguring sovereignty

The sovereignty of EU member states has been altered in practice to a far greater extent than that of those states which are merely caught up in the general interdependence of the globalised capitalist economy (Krasner 1999). Factors such as the contested but real strength and innovative character of EC law, the use of QMV, state liability for non-implementation of EU policy, and the adoption of the euro make this clear. Subsidiarity and flexibility further demonstrate through their presence on the Union agenda that European integration requires a new set of rules to guide the way in which member (and thus partner) states jointly exercise their powers as part of the democratisation of the Union system. These concepts speak to issues of balance between (sub/intra-)national and EU needs and responsibilities, to the scope of European integration, and to issues of civil society support for (and even participation in) EU governance. However, their truncated development to date also signals the real difficulties in creating this new set of rules through explicit choice, rather than in piecemeal fashion by an ongoing process of adopting half-measures.

Almost 50 years after the Treaty of Rome, national sovereignty remains very difficult to reconfigure explicitly in the EU context. The history of European integration has so far demonstrated the lack of will on the part of member states clearly to acknowledge the impact on their autonomy of their continuing membership of the EU, a political and economic system from which they retain the formal ability to secede, but only with enormous cost. This in turn indicates two problems whose importance cannot be underestimated. First, the likelihood that the member states do not really wish to address core issues of the democratic deficit (Warleigh 2002b). Second, the difficulty of justifying to the member state publics any attempt to address these issues, because this would require a frank admission of the real-world obsolescence of national sovereignty, a fiction which is strategically preserved even by the most famous pro-Europeans (witness Jacques Delors' illogical desire for the EU to be a 'federation of nation states').

Both subsidiarity and flexibility have in general been treated as pragmatic, or managerial, devices rather than normative principles in the elaboration of the Treaty over the last decade. Despite the reference at Maastricht to subsidiarity as a key norm of the EU in the Treaty Preamble, in practice it has been slowly transforming into proportionality ever since. With the Nice Treaty, flexibility has undergone a different trajectory – from unspoken, but common, practice to partially elaborated principle. However, at the time of writing both concepts meet at the mid-point of the governance tool – normative principle continuum, with a balance shift towards the latter being far from inevitable. Both concepts remain ambiguous and under-determined. This curtails their ability to help rectify the democratic deficit quite considerably.

Both flexibility and subsidiarity are capable of being represented as closet intergovernmentalism, and so appearing dangerous to actors who defend the traditional Community Method and its attendant state-like outcome. Subsidiarity, in this view, is a means to 'repatriate' EU competence, while flexibility represents the triumph of national governments' will over pan-EU solidarity. However, these concepts are also capable of representation as the expression of democratic values, denoting popular participation in decision-making, or at least the taking of decisions as closely to the people as possible (subsidiarity), and the respect for diversity rather than false homogeneity (flexibility). Thus, neither concept has an unclear relationship with democracy; there is no universal agreement about what they mean in the EU context, and no universal agreement about whether and how they could best be invoked as part of the Union's democratisation. Without sustained and frank deliberation of these issues, it is unlikely that either concept will be able to reach its potential.

The reconfiguration of national sovereignty in the EU remains disjointed: practice outstrips rhetoric to a very significant degree. To date, neither subsidiarity nor flexibility have been capable of addressing this problem, because they have been insufficiently elaborated and applied. The real heart of the matter – national sovereignty – has largely remained off limits as an issue of explicit debate. As a consequence, subsidiarity and flexibility have so far actually contributed to the democratic deficit, falsely reifying the idea that the issue was being addressed. In the next chapter I examine whether a similar failure to address the core of the problem has impacted on the utility of institutional reform as a strategy of democratic renewal in the EU.

NOTES

1   This is not to deny that they have a key difference: subsidiarity can be taken to imply a separation of powers which is universally agreed upon and uniformly operated; flexibility implies the opposite.
2   See Chapter 6 for a discussion of popular sovereignty and demos-formation in the EU.
3   It is of course largely for this reason that 'subsidiarity' and 'flexibility' are discussed instead.
4   For a trenchant criticism of the Court's reasoning, see Weiler 1995.
5   This reading of subsidiarity was advocated by the UK under the Major administration. The extent to which the subsequent governments have shared this view is a moot point.
6   Emiliou (1992: 404–6) argues subsidiarity is socio-political in nature, which appears to grant it greater leeway as a principle of EU governance. However, even for Emiliou, subsidiarity is not a legal or constitutional principle, but rather one which can best be used as a general reference point for political activity.
7   See below for a discussion of how this is not yet fully the case in practice.

4

Institutional Reform: The Paradoxical Case of the European Parliament

The Paradox of Power in the European Parliament

This chapter examines the impact on the democratic deficit of a key case of institutional reform, namely the rise to prominence of the European Parliament (EP). One of the most noticeable features of the EU's evolution has been its institutional creativity; over time new institutions and bodies have been created, and the powers of other institutions have been altered. The European Council, for example, was created to give leadership to the Union in the 1970s, thereby removing one of the Commission's tasks (Bulmer 1996). So, both the EU's institutional system and the relationships between the various institutions encompassed by it have been redefined at various stages in the integration process.[1] Moreover, this reconfiguration has often been motivated (at least in part) by explicit concerns to improve the EU's legitimacy, either as an efficient policy-maker or as a political system with greater representative and participatory capacities. A case in point is the establishment of the Committee of the Regions, whose weakness in fact serves to demonstrate the difficulties of such reform (Warleigh 2001e).

This chapter focuses on the European Parliament because it is the institution most commonly, and most interestingly, associated with the EU's democracy problem. Parliaments are expected to be important links to the citizen, with key tasks in the governance system; Mény and Knapp (1998: 182) list representation, decision and supervision/control of the executive as the main functions of parliaments in Western Europe. Thus, in terms of democratic theory, the EP is the most likely forum for the representation at EU level of the peoples rather than the governments of the member states: it is the body most likely to serve as a generator of, or repository for, direct supranational legitimacy – that is, legitimacy which is conferred on the supranational level directly by the citizen, without going through the mediating prism of national institutions. The EP's ability or otherwise to fulfil this function is a key indicator of the degree to which, and manner in which, the Union has developed beyond democracy defined as the collective expression of national will in the Council.

It is therefore of great significance that of all the Union institutions, it is the EP whose developmental trajectory is the most impressive. Over time, the EP has evolved from early days as a powerless assembly and acquired a highly significant degree of power as a legislator, budgetary authority and scrutiniser of the Commission. However, although the EP has been directly elected for over 20 years and conducts most of its meetings in public session, it remains bedevilled by a relatively low profile and the fact that it is less powerful than the Council in terms of making legislation. In fact, public interest in the EP has been steadily declining (Blondel et al., 1998) and despite its greater powers the EP appears to be no more able to socialise citizens into the EU system than before: the 1999 EP elections recorded the lowest voter turn-out since direct elections began in 1979. This is the great paradox of the European Parliament: significantly increased power, and a role in many ways more extensive than some national parliaments (Smith 1999), have not brought either it or the Union greater legitimacy.

In this chapter I argue that this paradox can be understood by focusing on how the EP exercises its newly-won legislative powers, since it is through this role in legislation that Parliament can both shape the *acquis* and impact upon the lives of EU citizens most extensively.[2] Building on Blondel et al. (1998: 10–11) I submit that the EP will only be considered to be a legitimate actor if it is empowered to act in policy areas which fulfil three criteria: they must be considered legitimate areas of supranational governance, areas in which democratic governance is necessary, and areas in which the EP, rather than other institutions or actors, is considered to be the best way to inject democracy into the EU system.[3]

It is important to focus on the EP's role as a legislator, and explore in particular the dynamics of the 'codecision' process, which marks its greatest gain in legislative power so far. I argue that codecision has empowered the Parliament significantly, but at the price of bringing it inside the very secretive system by which the EU makes policy, as a joint legislator with the Council. The Parliament (or at least many of its members) is now a key player in many if not most EU policy networks; but by the same token its influence usually goes unseen by the public, a fact which has compromised its ability to constitute a forum for public debate. The crucial stage of the codecision process, 'conciliation' (i.e. negotiations between Parliament and Council on how to resolve their differences over the proposed legislation), takes place behind closed doors. Moreover, because codecision requires the EP to adopt an agreed *institutional* perspective, and then enter it into a process of negotiation with the Council in order to produce an agreed *interinstitutional* legislative text, the EP is unable to develop patterns of partisan politics and meaningful plenary debate which might give it greater visibility.[4]

The structure of the chapter is as follows. In the next section, I explain the tasks and functions of the EP. I then examine the codecision procedure, and establish the extent to which, and means by which, it has empowered the Parliament. Finally, I use the criteria adapted from Blondel et al. (1998) to ask whether this empowerment has had a significant impact on the democratic deficit, and conclude that in these terms the undoubted transformation of the EP as a legislative force has been less than successful.

The powers of the European Parliament

As Burns (2001: 64) makes clear, the EP has five main formal powers which are impressive in scope, although it must be acknowledged at the outset that the EP possesses only a limited formal right of legislative initiative, and has far more powers to scrutinise the Commission than to oversee the Council.

- First, the Parliament has the ability to amend legislation, a power which can be used very extensively if the legal base of the legislation in question so permits.
- Second, the EP shares with the Council the responsibility to be the EU's budgetary authority (that is, to decide how the EU budget should be spent).
- Third, the EP has certain powers of scrutiny over the Commission, which include the right to grant discharge of the Union budget, the right to convene Committees of Inquiry into alleged maladministration in the implementation of EC law, and the right to ask questions of the Council and Commission.
- Fourth, the EP has powers of appointment over other EU bodies, such as the Ombudsman and, increasingly, the Commission.
- Fifth, the EP has the ability to dismiss the Commission as a whole body (although it cannot dismiss individual Commissioners).

These powers were not granted to the Parliament simultaneously; rather, they have been awarded to the EP over time. Neither Jean Monnet nor the member governments considered that a powerful Parliament was a necessary part of the EU system in its early stages (Smith 1999: 59). Instead, Parliament has been empowered on a gradual basis, beginning with the agreement by the member states that it should be directly elected as a response to the slowing down of the integration process in the 1970s and the attendant public Euroscepticism (Smith 1999: 48 and seq.). The EP has benefited over time from certain decisions of the ECJ on the issues of its powers and legal status, in particular in the Isoglucose case[5] (Bradley 1987, 1991), although the Court has by no means always made the judgments that Parliament wanted – notably over comitology issues (Weiler 1989). The Commission has also often been supportive of the EP's ambitions, perceiving that its own interests in terms of Commission-Council conflict could be bolstered by a stronger EP; thus, the Commission responded favourably to the cooperation procedure, accepting the great majority of amendments proposed by the EP (Corbett 1989; Van Hamme 1988). Parliament has also been adroit in exploiting its powers in order to facilitate its own development, by such mechanisms as seeking to influence the Commission's legislative agenda by the issue of own initiative reports, dialogue between key MEPs and other actors at national and EU levels, and prioritising action in policy areas where the legal base affords the EP its maximum formal power (Earnshaw and Judge 1995; Judge 1992; Judge and Earnshaw 1994).

In formal terms, however, the EP obviously owes its expanded powers to Treaty change, and consequently to the collective will of the member governments (Moravcsik 1999). Parliament's powers over the budget originate in the Budget Treaties of 1970 and 1975. The EP's legislative role has grown since direct elections to it were first held in 1979, with each subsequent revision to the EU Treaties expanding its ability to influence EU legislation through the creation, revision and extension of new legislative procedures. The Single European Act (SEA), for example, introduced the cooperation procedure, which gave the Parliament the right to a second reading of proposed legislation and the ability to reject it by absolute majority (although a unanimous Council could overturn this rejection). The assent procedure was also introduced by the SEA. This gave the Parliament the ability to veto legislation after a single reading, but not to amend the proposal; 'assent' is an all-or-nothing procedure. Both these new procedures applied to very few areas of policy, although among those areas covered by the cooperation procedure was the single market, a key EU policy area (Burns 2001). The Maastricht Treaty gave Parliament the ability to set up committees of inquiry, introduced the codecision procedure, and gave Parliament a consultative vote of confidence in the appointment of the Commission President and the individual Commissioners. The Amsterdam Treaty streamlined the codecision procedure, extended its use to further areas of policy, and formalised the EP's role in the Commission appointment process. The Nice Treaty slightly extended the use of codecision and reinforced the legal standing of the Parliament vis-à-vis the Council and

Commission (European Parliament 2001). Thus, the EP is now a powerful institution, with sufficient confidence to force the resignation of the Santer-led Commission in 1999.[6]

The impact of codecision

The most important stage in this process of development – in terms of the EP's ability to carry legislative influence – was the establishment of the codecision procedure. This process, established at Maastricht, then refined at Amsterdam, makes the Parliament and Council roughly equal as legislators. In its original variant, codecision gave both EP and Council two readings of the proposal, and provided for a process known as conciliation if the two institutions could not agree on the content of legislation. The goal of the conciliation process (held with only Parliament and Council as formal negotiators) was to produce a 'joint text', which would then be approved by both institutions. If conciliation failed, the Council could impose its own view (the 'Common Position' of the member states), unless the EP rejected it by an absolute majority, in which case there would be no legislation. Thus, the nub of the issue was the incentive to negotiate: would Parliament be able to generate absolute majorities whenever Council sought to impose its own Common Position, and thereby fight fire with fire? Would the Council put the EP to the test, or simply assume that its Common Position would always be a bargaining position rather than an unchangeable legislative text? In short, would the two institutions, traditionally seen to represent opposing interests, be able to act as co-legislators?

As revised at Amsterdam, codecision is a streamlined process, with the emphasis still on conciliation but with the ability of the Council to impose its Common Position removed. Thus, if conciliation fails, there is no legislation, and both institutions are under greater pressure to reach an agreement. The Amsterdam Treaty also enabled this agreement to be made after both institutions have had their first reading of the proposal; if Council and EP can agree at that stage, there is now no need to undertake the second readings and conciliation. This facilitates the development of a joint legislative culture between EP and Council, which was already incipient as a result of the Maastricht Treaty (Shackleton 2000). In addition, the Amsterdam Treaty applied codecision to a far wider range of policy areas, covering most of the first pillar (Maurer 1999).[7]

In the academic debate, codecision has been controversial on three main counts.

- First, it has been questioned whether the procedure really empowers the Parliament, or whether it is an elaborate mechanism by which the member states retain all meaningful power while weakening the Commission (Garrett and Tsebelis 1996; Moravcsik 1999).

- Second, it has been contended that a meaningful transfer of power to the EP did occur, but at Amsterdam rather than at Maastricht (Tsebelis and Garrett 2001).

- Third, it has been suggested that the empowerment of the EP, at least regarding the post-Amsterdam variant of codecision, is a risk for the EU system because it makes 'indecision' (the failure to agree legislation) more likely (Crombez 2001).

Moravcsik's account of codecision is a useful illustration of the first school of thought. In this view (Moravcsik 1999) codecision is a deliberate tactic to dissolve the traditional, if by no means always reliable, alliance between the EP and the Commission by a strategy of divide-and-rule. For Moravcsik, codecision represents not so much a transfer of sovereignty from national to EU level, but rather a redistribution of the powers already delegated to the Union by the member states in favour of the EP and to the detriment of the Commission. This was done by reducing the power of the Commission to reject amendments proposed by the EP, and by making it far easier for Parliament to negotiate directly with Council. Moravcsik argues that it is important to remember the limited scope of codecision: and indeed, even after Nice, it still does not apply across the board, and it does nothing to reduce the Commission's formal near-monopoly on the right of legislative initiative in the first pillar.

Moravcsik's arguments hold at least some water. Westlake (1994) points out that MEPs were initially wary of codecision, some of them considering that the Maastricht variant left Council in the dominant position. Dankert (1997) argues that the main policy areas to which the procedure initially applied – those relating to the single market – reduced the importance of codecision, not because this policy area is unimportant but because the bulk of the relevant legislation was already in place. Moreover, as pointed out by Dinan (1997), codecision did nothing to reduce the use of comitology, meaning that EP influence over the general content of legislation might be outweighed by the influence wielded by national experts sitting on the relevant technical committees.[8]

Other commentators (Garrett and Tsebelis 1996; Tsebelis et al. 2001) have argued that the Maastricht codecision in fact undermined both the Commission and the EP. According to Garrett and Tsebelis (1996) the EP's veto power was very unlikely to be used (in fact, it was used in the case of the 1994 Voice Telephony directive), because a majority of MEPs would prefer almost any legislation to a legislative vacuum, in order to boost the *acquis communautaire*. Therefore those actors likely to be really empowered by codecision were those national governments whose preferences were close to the EP view, and who could use the threat of an EP veto as a device to generate a Council position which reflected their own stance.[9] Tsebelis et al. (2001) argue that (at least under the Maastricht regime) the EP did less well under codecision than it had under the cooperation procedure, because it was obliged under cooperation to make effective interinstitutional partnerships. These partnerships with actors in the Commission and Council were likely to give the EP more influence, more often, because they represented a joint position of many stakeholders rather than a unilateral stance adopted by the Parliament as a sole actor – even if that influence was limited by the constraints of the partnership. Tsebelis et al. (2001) cite survey evidence that in fact Council rejected proportionately far fewer amendments under cooperation than under codecision.

However, such views are not universally shared. Corbett (1998) notes that both EP and Council made practical arrangements to smooth the operation of codecision from the outset. Garman and Hilditch (1998) demonstrate that Parliament, Commission and Council all learned to make the conciliation process function successfully with remarkable speed, laying particular emphasis on the informal meetings (known as 'trialogues') between key actors from each institution, which enable negotiations to progress 'behind the scenes' and then receive formal approval in the conciliation delegation meetings. Scully (1997) has argued that conciliation often works to the advantage of the EP, since its delegation is far more flexible than that of the Council, whose members are perpetually obliged to refer back to their national capitals for guidance. Thus, it can be easier for the EP to provide brokers and policy entrepreneurs than the Council, in the context of conciliation, which means that the EP is more likely than Council to generate an interinstitutional compromise solution in its favour. Maurer (1999) argues that the EP's efforts to capitalise on codecision have led it to create a small team of 'permanent members' of conciliation delegations, who have developed special expertise in the conciliation process. In turn, this has helped the EP ensure that almost 60% of its amendments at second reading of a proposal are either accepted by Council or form the basis for compromise texts in conciliation (Maurer 1999). Quantity is not necessarily quality; but Earnshaw and Judge (1996) found that even in the early days of codecision the EP was able to help produce legislation which was significantly different from both the Commission's proposal and the Council's Common Position.

Most tellingly, Shackleton (2000) argues that codecision has in fact altered the entire relationship between Parliament and Council. The two institutions try to identify likely problems before conciliation begins, in order to solve them speedily. Institutional trust has developed, in that actors from both institutions expect their counterparts to be prepared to negotiate and to deliver ratification of the compromise text. Indeed, Shackleton even argues that conciliation can cast a shadow in front of itself: in the case of the 1998 Biotechnology Directive, it was not necessary to go beyond first reading of the proposal in either Parliament or Council, because Council took on board already at that stage all Parliament's main concerns. Thus, even the anticipation of conciliation can sometimes be sufficient to create a joint legislative culture between the Council and Parliament. Where compromise it not reached this easily, EP actors can work alongside national politicians and a range of other actors to secure their objectives as part of a 'policy coalition', exploiting the codecision system as appropriate (Warleigh 2000a). Thus, even under the conditions set by the Maastricht Treaty, it seems clear that codecision had a significant impact on the EP's ability to influence policy outcomes.

The second school of thought – that codecision has empowered the EP, but only as a result of the Amsterdam Treaty – is advanced by Tsebelis and Garrett (2001). Their concern that the EP would in fact lose influence under codecision (by being lured into the abandonment of the pursuit of interinstitutional partnerships in favour of an unusable veto, which Council could in any case trump) was mitigated by the Amsterdam Treaty provision for conciliation to be the absolute end of the decision making process. In this reading, the EP's loss of its veto is small beer compared with Council's loss of the ability to impose its Common Position, thereby forcing the EP to try to oppose it by absolute majority, because Council unanimity is considered more likely than the generation of an absolute majority in the EP. Consequently, both institutions have an incentive to enter into conciliation negotiations with a constructive purpose, and the likelihood of the EP being constantly unable to secure its objectives is reduced. Pollack (1999) notes that this transcends the view that the member states and EP have a principal-agent relationship, because after Amsterdam Parliament has legislative powers whose use the member states cannot control, even as a collective.

The third line of argument is put forward by Crombez (2001), who maintains that although the Amsterdam Treaty makes clear the rise of Parliament to a position of joint legislator with Council in most legislation of the first pillar, this ascent has been mismanaged. Crombez argues along almost diametrically opposed lines to Garrett and Tsebelis. He submits that Amsterdam actually makes it more difficult for Parliament to secure its objectives because the Commission rather than the Council is weakened considerably, and conciliation has become an all-or-nothing process: if it fails, there is no legislation. Given that there is no fall-back position, and that the Commission's ability to broker agreement between the negotiators is much reduced (because EP and Council negotiate directly), Crombez fears Parliament may find itself in a bind. If the EP cannot reach a suitable compromise with Council, it will have to choose between two unpalatable options: either agreeing to legislation it does not really want, or accepting a legislative vacuum. Either way, the outcome would be suboptimal. However, it is not clear why Parliament should be more vulnerable in this way than Council. Moreover, it is by no means certain, given the experience of codecision to date, that the threat of an expanding legislative vacuum is real. In fact, given Shackleton's findings mentioned above, it appears that such an eventuality is unlikely.

So, it is clear that codecision has empowered the EP and unleashed a novel kind of interinstitutional politics of decision-making in which Parliament and Council are moving closer together, while the Commission is playing a lesser role. This trend is by no means irreversible, but it relies on dynamics which appear to be solidly established. Started at Maastricht, and imperfectly cast, codecision relied upon concerted effort by Parliament and Council to be operationalised successfully, and generated a set of informal practices which meant that it could work to the benefit of the EP. Formalised in part at Amsterdam, these innovations mean that '(t)oday the EU looks very much like a traditional ... bicameral legislature' (Tsebelis and Garrett 2001: 374). It remains to discuss the impact these changes have made on the democratic deficit.

The persistent democratic deficit: power, not legitimacy, for the European Parliament?

The shallowness of the assumption that the EP's acquisition of greater status would automatically bring it greater legitimacy and public resonance has long been established. It is no surprise therefore that its acquisition of greater powers should have a similarly low public impact. Direct elections to Parliament are a very instructive example. For federalists, direct elections have been a disappointment, in that despite obtaining a direct link to the public which no other EU institution could rival the EP did not emerge as an institution with greater legitimacy. As Lodge and Herman (1982) point out, even the first EP elections failed to make a significant public impact, with little consideration given by national governments to such issues as how links should be made between national and European parliaments. Indeed, national governments often treated elected MEPs no differently from their appointed predecessors, with national rather than European issues dominating the election campaigns. Futhermore, there were few signs of European commonality, given the 'absence of a common electoral law, common election day, common parties capable of contesting the elections, common provisions regarding voter eligibility' and the lack of common rules on electoral campaigning (Lodge and Herman 1982: 265). This established a trend which shows no sign of changing after more than 20 years, although there is now agreement in all member states that EP elections must use some form of proportional representation, and the Maastricht Treaty gives member state nationals the right to vote and stand in EP elections in their member state of residence rather than the member state whose nationality they possess, as part of the provisions on EU citizenship. Direct elections have made little impact on the political consciousness of EU citizens; their general lack of interest in the EP has been clear for almost two decades (Sonntag and Featherstone 1984).

In fact, the *impact of direct elections was actually felt at the supranational level rather than at that of the general publics of the member states.* Direct elections made Parliament more assertive in its relations with Council (Smith 1999: 59–60; Sonntag and Featherstone 1984). In the 'Brussels village',[10] direct elections enabled Parliament to claim the legitimacy necessary to reject EU budgets, propose EU reforms which were partially taken up in subsequent treaty revisions (Spinelli's Draft Treaty on European Union being a case in point) and gradually to use the legislative powers it was granted to the fullest extent possible. However, outside Brussels, the role played by the EP is little understood. This is a crucial factor, because it encapsulates the EP's dilemma very succinctly. MEPs and Parliament as a whole have been more than capable of using their powers in a variety of ways to influence the EU agenda or shape its legislative output, but they have done so in a near vacuum of public interest and knowledge. This is partly because the EU as a whole has often suffered from lack of public interest and even scepticism. It is also because national governments remain reluctant to explain how much power has actually been given to the EP (Smith 1999).

Of course, it cannot be assumed that EU citizens would automatically support such a transfer of power; but it is reasonable to suppose that greater general understanding of the EP's influence would foster greater levels of participation in its elections. Even here, however, the case is not clear: the 1999 EP elections followed quickly after the very public Commission resignation scandal in which the EP played a vital role, and yet voter turnout levels fell again (Lambert and Hoskyns 2000). There may be dangers for Parliament in such activity, given the general climate of Euroscepticism which appears to lead voters into criticism of the EU as a whole, rather than disapprobation of specific institutions: voters are not sufficiently socialised into the EU system to separate out dissatisfaction with particular parts of it from dissatisfaction with the system in its entirety (Warleigh 2001c). Thus, particularly when the EP itself often faces criticism that it is a 'gravy train', it is not evident that the EP will always get the credit for using its powers extensively – although not to use them would invite justifiable accusations of weakness (Neunreither 2000b).

There is yet another complicating factor which must be examined: the fact that the EP instantiates a different kind of parliamentary politics from that which nationals of many member states consider to operate within their state. As a result, the EP fails to register as a 'parliament' with many EU citizens – despite the fact that the EP now carries out significant tasks under all three functions listed by Mény and Knapp (1998) as those central to parliamentary powers. For example, the EP is not the source of an EU 'government',[11] and although the political party groups of the EP play a key role in its functioning (Burns 2001), the Europeanisation of political parties as a whole remains low (Lord 1998b). Media coverage of, and interest in, the EP remains generally low, and the public profile of most of its members is equally unimpressive, despite the fact that many MEPs are skilful and talented politicians. Thus, many of the tools used to bind the public to national political systems and parliaments are less easy to use at EU level.

The problem here is that the EP represents very clearly the phenomenon that Andersen and Burns (1996: 229–48) have called 'post-parliamentary governance'; given the lack of general socialisation into the EU system, its incarnation of a phenomenon common to most Western European political systems (Steiner 1998) is more evident than the presence of such changes at national level. According to the 'post-parliamentary governance' thesis, all modern polities increasingly derive their legitimacy from expertise rather than direct representation of the public. The complexity and increased scope of contemporary policy-making, together with its increasing reliance on international frameworks and standards, means that elected politicians are decreasingly able to contribute to, or even adequately monitor, decision-making processes which either take place outside the national jurisdictions in which they are empowered or demand detailed knowledge which they lack. Although this kind of system may produce policies which are successful as a result of their expert formulation, it has problematic accountability and transparency because neither electors nor elected politicians are always able to control the real decision makers.

In member states, this phenomenon is characterised by the general shift to the executive, while in the EU this trend is reflected in the pre-eminence of the Council. However, national decision-making takes place in an arena with which most citizens identify strongly, and in which familiar institutions remain visible; EU decision-making does not have this luxury, even if many member state nationals accept it as a useful policy-making device (Banchoff and Smith 1999). Thus, the EP, as a relatively new institution whose powers do not correspond exactly to the liberal democratic template of what constitutes a parliament, is particularly vulnerable to criticism and scepticism. This problem is compounded by the fact that *national* parliaments appear to have been weakened by the European integration process: the Council bargains in secret, which makes it difficult for national parliaments to scrutinise the behaviour of national ministers (Chryssochoou et al. 1998).[12] It is thus of great potential significance that the 'constitutional convention' set up by the Laeken summit to inform IGC 2004 has as one of its principal agenda items the relationship between national parliaments and the EU/EP.

However, the issue of scrutiny of the use of public power is also of relevance in another, very complex way: the impact of codecision. Because conciliation means that Council and EP must agree a joint text, Parliament can oblige national ministers as a collective to agree upon legislation which they might otherwise have opposed at the express order of their national parliaments. This is not a merely an abstract issue as it speaks directly to the issues of popular sovereignty discussed in Chapter 3: if national parliaments and the EP are in conflict, which should prevail, and why? The EP's legislative power on any issue, it must ultimately be recalled, is not primarily the result of transparency or public debate, but rather is the result of Parliament's entry into the metaphorical 'smoke-filled rooms' in which EU policy deals are negotiated and bargained *in camera* (Lambert and Hoskyns 2000). As co-legislator in a way which is different from most national parliaments, the EP's independence as a scrutineer of both Council and Commission in their respective roles is not clear-cut.

Furthermore, codecision has empowered Parliament in a way which truncates its ability to reach out to civil society (Lambert and Hoskyns 2000). As an institution, the EP has significant legislative power; but because it has to wield this power through (or in anticipation of) the conciliation process, the ability to translate greater importance into a higher public profile is severely limited. Conciliation empowers the EP committee which had primary responsibility for the EP report in question, as its members constitute the bulk of the EP conciliation delegation; in particular, the Committee Chairperson and Rapporteur are likely to play a very significant role (Collins et al. 1998; Warleigh 2000b). This does not equate to an increase in public debate about EU policy, or greater opportunities for EU citizens to make a transparent impact on EU policy via their elected representatives. Indeed, given that the EP conciliation delegation has to form a unified position and promise to deliver on any agreed bargain in order to strike a deal with Council, the scope for meaningful public debate in the EP may actually have decreased (Lambert and Hoskyns 2000).

Conclusions

The EP's increased powers have not signalled a clear improvement in the EU's democratic credentials. In fact, it is the European Court of Justice rather than the EP which appears to be the institution most trusted by member state nationals to represent their interests at EU level (Blondel et al. 1998: 119). This should not be surprising if we recall the criteria set out in the introduction of this chapter, namely that the EP could only be considered an actor likely to increase the EU's perceived legitimacy if:

- it acts in policy areas the public considers appropriate for transnational governance;
- it acts in areas which the public also considers to be appropriate for democratic governance;
- it acts in areas in which the EP, rather than other actors or institutions, is considered by the public to be the most appropriate vehicle for such democratic governance.

That the EP is now joint legislator in most areas falling under the first pillar is not in itself proof it meets the first criterion, given the mismatch between what surveys indicate the public wants the EU to do, and the tasks with which it is actually entrusted (Blondel et al. 1998). As pointed out by Everts and Sinnott (1995) support for the EU appears to have been in over-all decline since 1991. According to Gabel (1998b), the real level of public support for European integration may be much lower than previously assumed, if we take as an indicator not those who profess any degree of support for the Union (the traditional approach) but rather those who declare strong attachment to it. Thus, although this is not within the powers of the EP to change, Parliament may be acting in areas in which suprana-tional governance itself is considered illegitimate by many citizens.

The second criterion is similarly difficult for the EP on two grounds. First, as a corollary of the point made immediately above, the Parliament may be inactive in areas which the public does consider suitable for demo-cratic (supranational) governance. For example, Eurobarometer data sur-veyed by Blondel et al. (1998: 67) indicates that of the ten issue areas most regularly considered by citizens to be suitable for the EU rather than national governments to be the main actor, in only one case – environment policy – does the EP play a significant legislative role. Second, even when the EP is active in an issue area considered appropriate, there is no guaran-tee that it will be so in a way which either proves its instrumental utility to the citizen or serves to increase their knowledge of it – as demonstrated by the curate's egg that is the codecision process.

The third criterion is perhaps the most difficult of all. Most citizens continue to focus on (sub)national actors and institutions, rather than those at EU level, as the locus of democratic governance. Where there is an agree-ment that democratic governance is necessary at EU level, it is entirely coherent, although not the view advocated here, to argue from a commu-nitarian perspective that this means all power should rest in the hands of the Council, perhaps ultimately depending on the member state veto power. From a different perspective, it could be argued that bodies other than

Parliament serve best to represent societal interests in EU forums: this argument was made about the Economic and Social Committee (ESC) in the early days of the EU (Zellentin 1962), and more recently, as part of a radical rethinking of EU democracy (Abromeit 1998). Given that there are multiple possibilities for representing citizens' interests in the EU system, and ensuring that they shape the legislation produced by it (Lord 1998a), it cannot be assumed that the EP would be the citizen's automatic choice of representative actor.

Thus, the EP's ascent to legislative power has not been a means by which the 'democratic deficit' has been clearly reduced. Formally speaking, the legitimacy of the Union has been enhanced to the extent that it now has a single electorate in terms of EP elections, and those elections are direct. However, the Union remains a system of 'post-parliamentary governance', if by that we mean one in which executive power and the politics of expertise (comitology) are clearly at the apex of the system. Moreover, the EP is obliged to wield its new powers in a manner which both conceptually and practically removes it from the public view, through the intricacies of the codecision process. Therefore, in terms of substantive democracy, its new powers are far less impressive than they are in terms of formal democracy; Parliament is ultimately an institution through which skilful MEPs can wield substantial influence, but not a body in which citizens can experience making their voices heard. In the next chapter I ask whether reform of another kind – increasing the policy scope and competence of the EU – offers grounds for a different conclusion.

NOTES

1   For an overview, see the essays in Warleigh (2001e).

2   Another important issue is obviously that of representation: do EU citizens feel that the EP is 'their' institution, one which represents them collectively as a demos? The issue of demos-formation is addressed in Chapter 6, and so is not tackled here.

3   Blondel et al. (1998) list the first two criteria. I have added the third to ensure greater specificity.

4   There are some indications that this may be changing (Hix 2001); the impact of the EP's President, Pat Cox, who was elected in January 2002, will be a key indicator here.

5   This ruling stated that the Council is obliged to wait for the EP to issue an opinion before it can legislate, even under the consultation procedure (which allows Parliament only one reading and no ability to insist Council takes its opinion into account). This gave Parliament its first real influence, because the EP was thereby effectively empowered to hold up the legislative process if it considered changes necessary to a given proposal (Burns 2001).

6 Formally, the Commission resigned before it could be dismissed by the EP, an action which otherwise would certainly have occurred.

7 Maurer (1999: 43) cites various estimates that after Amsterdam, 70% of EU legislation would be covered by the codecision procedure, although he cautions that this may be an excessive estimate.

8 However, as pointed out by Garman and Hilditch (1998), the EP has in fact used conciliation negotiations to raise the issue of comitology and secure certain changes. Burns (2001) points out that since 1999, the EP and Council have agreed a modus operandi on comitology.

9 Of course, it is hard to imagine how some member states would be able to perceive the supposedly false nature of the EP veto threat while others would not, especially given that the set of member states with preferences close to those of the EP would in all likelihood change according to the issue at hand, and thus most if not all member states would be in the position to learn from experience.

10 Brussels functions increasingly as the capital of the EU political system, with an international political class dominating the city. As with other major political cities, Brussels generates its own small world of politicians, lobbyists, officials, embassies and consultants in its role as de facto EU capital as well as that of the Belgian federation. The EP plays a full part in this 'Brussels' system, despite the fact that it is obliged by the member states to hold many of its plenary sessions in Strasbourg.

11 As Lord (1998a) points out, this is not a function of parliaments in all European countries. I cite it here merely as an example of a key parliamentary function in systems such as that of the UK.

12 It should be noted that national parliaments have often responded vigorously to this problem, setting up effective scrutiny committees and retaining their position as the ultimate ratifiers of Treaty change. National parliaments do not have much influence on EU decision-making as such, but they can nevertheless be important actors in EU affairs via their influence on national governments (Raunio 1999; Raunio and Hix 2001).

5

Increasing EU Scope and Powers: The Cases of Environment and Regional Policies

In this chapter I examine the impact upon the EU's legitimacy of its acquisition of significant competence in two key areas of policy: the environment and regional development. According to neofunctionalists, growth in the EU's powers can be expected to increase popular support for the Union: put simply, a Union capable of doing more for its citizens is expected to meet more of their aspirations, thereby demonstrating its relevance and utility, and encouraging more and more individuals and groups to engage with, or at least lend their support to, the integration process. However, one of the most intriguing paradoxes of the EU's democracy crisis is that this assumption appears to have been almost entirely misplaced. After 50 years of evolution from the days of the Coal and Steel Community, the Union now has competence in vital policy areas such as the single currency, defence, and foreign policy, not to mention the single market: nobody could reasonably question its centrality in the political processes of all its member states, and even of many states which have yet to join (Schmitter 1996a, 1996b). Nonetheless, the issue of the 'democratic deficit' has blighted the integration process far more over the last decade than previously.

This juxtaposition of increased policy competence with decreased, or at least more closely questioned, legitimacy can partly be explained by examining issues of subsidiarity and demos-formation (see Chapters 3 and 6). If the EU develops competence in issue areas which citizens consider inappropriate for transnational governance, its new powers are likely to decrease rather than augment its perceived legitimacy (Blondel et al. 1998). However, there are other factors which also need to be considered. First, not all EU powers have accrued according to either explicit choice or sustained strategic interests, clearly explicated and justified to the citizen. In fact, certain EU competences have been added (or resisted) by member governments for domestic political reasons, producing an unbalanced set of EU competences which include a commitment to promote animal welfare, but exclude many of the measures necessary to make a reality of the rhetoric of EU citizenship, thereby reducing the ability of the individual to take advantage of the single market (see the essays in Bellamy and Warleigh 2001). Second, other policies and even institutions have been created as a result of opportunistic action by the member states and EU institutions, seeking to add to the Union's scope wherever possible rather than according to a logical overall strategy (see the essays in Warleigh 2001e). So, the EU has not developed into a polity where power is wielded according to either a logical and transparent division of powers or a clear, informed choice by member governments and their citizens about what the EU should do, and how.

However, even these three considerations do not suffice to produce a holistic explanation of why the EU's increase in powers has not added significantly to its perceived legitimacy, because in certain policy areas the EU *has* acquired competences in a way which is broadly in line with public expectations of the policy-making role it should undertake. According to Blondel et al. (1998: 67) both environmental protection and reducing the disparities between the regions of the EU are consistently rated by citizens as areas in which the Union should be active. The EU's growth of significant competence in these policy areas since the 1970s should be of help in addressing its legitimacy problem. Perhaps especially for those on the left of the political spectrum, both sustainability and social cohesion – the current cornerstones of environmental and regional policies respectively – are important principles which could invigorate EU governance both normatively and substantively. This is because both policies have a redistributive, market-correcting element, and thereby aim to reduce social inequalities. They certainly help demonstrate to the citizen that the EU can produce significant benefits in terms of successful public policy, generating stronger output legitimacy for the Union. They also focus on issues of participation, helping present the EU as 'more than a market' and building participatory capacity in both the NGO sector and, especially through the 'partnership principle' of regional policy, across a range of social partners, local authoristies and civil society groups. Thus, both these policies should be able to increase the Union's input legitimacy. Furthermore, since the 1999 reforms, environmental protection has to some extent been integrated as part of the logic of regional policy, with a specific fund – LIFE – created to reflect this (Barnes and Barnes 1999). Accordingly, the potential of environmental and regional policies to add to the legitimacy of the Union is high: the two policy areas are developed in a fair degree of harmony with each other, and aim to change both the market emphasis of the Union and its inadequately participatory political culture.

Nonetheless, I argue in this chapter that this potential largely remains to be realised. The EU is a significant actor in both environmental and regional policies, and has certainly been able to demonstrate the capacity to act according to the expressed wishes of its citizens in these issue areas. That said, environmental policy faces significant problems of non-implementation, and is also undergoing a change from regulation to soft policy which arguably reduces its capacity to improve the conditions of the European environment. Moreover, much of the justification for EU environment policy – the truism that pollution knows no frontiers – can also be applied to the more broadly international arena, and at this level the EU is less effective than it might be in securing strong policy agreements between itself and non-member states such as the USA. Regional policy remains attached to a very small budget, albeit one which has dramatically increased as a proportion of the EU budget over time. Thus, the Union's ability to reduce regional disparities is rather limited. Furthermore, there is a mounting body of evidence that the local-level partnerships which are supposed to play a key role in the making of regional policy remain under the control of central governments, thereby frustrating the potential of 'partnership' to create opportunities for participation and socialization into the EU system. Taken together, these problems present a significant impediment to the EU's ability to generate greater legitimacy for itself by increasing its policy scope even in issue areas where it is widely held to be a legitimate actor. The evidence from environmental and regional policies indicates that the Union has real difficulty in adding a significant ecological or social democratic element to its market-making core activities. To this extent there is no automatic 'spillover' between public perceptions of the Union's greater utility or competence and public perceptions of its legitimacy (Bellamy and Warleigh 1998).

The structure of the chapter is as follows. First, I examine environment policy, charting its history as an EU competence and analysing its key principles and problems. Second, I undertake the same task in the field of regional policy. Finally, I draw conclusions about the capacity of these policies to increase the EU's perceived legitimacy.

EU environment policy: origins and principles

EU competence in environment policy has developed over time by a series of fascinating mechanisms. Initially without any specific competence in this policy field, the Union nevertheless made a surprising amount of environmental legislation through the use of the Treaty of Rome (1957) provisions to ensure harmonious economic development of the member states and a qualitative improvement of citizens' standards of living (Marin 1997). Indeed, the EU has had environmental action plans ever since 1973, despite the fact that its first specific legal competence to act to protect the environment came with the SEA in the mid-1980s (Lévêque 1996c). Perhaps unsurprisingly, this ability to make policy without explicit Treaty provision, and then capitalise upon Treaty sanction, has led to environmental policy developing a set of political dynamics of its own: it is an entrepreneurial policy regime and arena (Zito 2000) which is widely considered to be one of the EU's most successful policies (Judge 1993), one of its most important in terms of supranational reach into member state structures (Sbragia 2000) and one which epitomises the Union's ability to undertake a meaningful role in the international political economy (Zito 2000).

The growth of EU competence in environment policy can be attributed to two main factors. First, several member states with strong national policies on environmental protection have sought to ensure that actors and firms from their own territories were not disadvantaged as a result of participation in the single market (Sbragia 2000). A German firm obliged to incorporate pollution costs into its prices to customers, for example, is likely to charge more than a Greek company under no such obligation; this might give the Greek firm an advantage in the context of the single market if consumers prioritise goods according mainly to price. To avoid inflicting losses on domestic firms, therefore, German governments have tended to support an EU role in environment policy which can ensure that all firms have to incorporate similar environmental legislation. As Marin (1997: 580–2) points out, however, there is an important second factor to remember here: by and large, member states did not seek to establish fair competition by removing environmental policy considerations, as might have been the more obvious choice given the EU's general development trajectory, but rather by creating new environmental protection standards at EU level. Thus, there is a part to be played by ideas and beliefs in explaining how the EU has come to have an extensive environmental policy; member states wanted to protect their domestic industries, but also to respond to public concerns about both environmental degradation and the role of the EU. (This also helps explain why EU environment policy is not internally coherent: according to Zito (2000: 6), politics rather than scientific expertise informs the core of Union action on the environment, meaning that this policy reflects changing bargains and beliefs rather than a clear and consistent set of scientific values/approaches.) Nevertheless, most scholars agree that the essential reason for the EU's acquisition of significant competence in environmental policy was the creation of the single market (Barnes and Barnes 1999; Van der Straaten 1993; Weale and Williams 1993). It does seem significant that it was the Single European Act, dedicated to the

completion of the single market, which provided the EU with its first clear
legal base for action in environment policy (Weale and Williams 1993); as
with so much in European integration, environment policy could be
advanced as a flanking measure to support the process of market-making
and 'prevent the distortion of trade' (Barnes and Barnes 1999: 11).

As Collins (1997) elaborates, there are three core principles of EU
environment policy: that prevention of environmental damage is better than
cure (the 'precautionary principle'); that in cases of such damage, the
polluter should pay for remedial action (the 'polluter pays' principle); and
that the Union must integrate the principle of sustainable development into
all its policies, i.e. not just those which are obviously 'environmental', but
others such as the rapid reaction force or single currency (the 'sustainability' principle). The first of these principles is intended to reduce environmental damage by preventing actors from undertaking activities which are
likely to cause environmental harm. The second is intended as a deterrent,
so that polluters know that they will be obliged to make financial repara-
tions for their behaviour. The third, embodied by the Amsterdam Treaty, is
considered the key to making the first two effective: by integrating
environmental considerations into the design of all EU policies, it is intended
that degradation of natural resources will be minimised and that economic
growth can be made compatible with resource conservation.

Despite the existence of these clear principles, however, the actual content of environment policy at EU level is difficult to characterise because, as
Knill (2001:121) demonstrates, it is composed not of a single approach but
rather of several different policy instruments and rationales. Although these
different approaches collectively make EU action in this area extensive, they
also mean that this action is rather fragmented. For example, drinking
water policy is subject to binding legislation which prescribes maximum
permissible levels of pollution; ecolabelling policy relies upon firms
perceiving advantage in voluntary compliance with standards of good
environmental practice.[1] Moreover, despite the existence of such legislation
as the Birds and Habitats Directives, and the Environmental Impact
Assessment Directive, EU environmental legislation is centred on the prevention of pollution rather than more ecologically ambitious objectives
(Marin 1997).

The making of EU environment policy: legitimacy
through inclusion or 'sound science'?

Environment policy simultaneously exemplifies both that the Union is much
more than the tool of the 'big' member states, and also how national governments can nonetheless significantly influence the everyday level of

policy-making as well as the 'history-making' decisions of Treaty-creation and reform (to use Peterson's 1995 typology). This is because of two contrasting factors. First, the process by which environment policy is made is fundamentally political rather than technocratic, involving contestation of the means and objectives of proposals both between the member states, and between the Council and the other institutions (Lévêque 1996b; Zito 2000). Zito, in fact, shows that the 'small' member states, EP and extra-EU frameworks such as those of the OECD can have a significant impact upon EU environmental policy, a finding mirrored by Judge (1993) in his treatment of the role played in this area by the EP and its committees. The fact that the EP has long been granted its largest influence in environment policy is significant here, because over time Parliament and its environment committee have developed extensive expertise in exploiting the powers they enjoy under the cooperation and codecision procedures (see Chapter 4). Indeed, the Amsterdam Treaty ensured that codecision would be the norm in environment policy-making, which should both help the EP maximise its legislative influence and further open up the possibilities for participation in the relevant coalitions and networks by EP actors, NGOs, civil society groups and those from 'green' industry (Sbragia 2000; Warleigh 2000b; Webster 1998). Thus, environment policy is an area in which the EU is not only commonly perceived to be a legitimate actor, but one in which diverse non-state actors and structures are frequently influential.

The second factor, however, is the fact that by the time they reach the statute book, the Commission's proposals for environmental legislation are often far less 'green' than when they were initiated. This is generally taken to indicate persistent member state will and ability to dilute the proposals' impact and costs (Lévêque 1996a), despite what scholars have identified as often strong partnerships between the EP and Commission in this area (Judge 1993). Therefore, the contribution of the mechanics of policy-making to the ability of environment policy to increase the EU's input legitimacy is problematised – the Union is unlikely to appear legitimate to actors who are encouraged to participate in decision-making but find themselves blocked by recalcitrant member states or other actors.[2]

Moreover, this fundamentally political nature of environmental policy-making reduces the Union's ability to claim output legitimacy based on the use of scientific data to inform policy. 'Sound science' is by no means always at the heart of EU environment policy, which may well result from bargaining and compromise between different coalitions of actors, thereby reflecting the 'politics of the possible' (or what can be constructed as necessary) rather than what scientists or environmentalists would argue constitute the logical parameters of policy (Marin 1997). So, the presence of many non-state actors in EU environment policy networks does not automatically equate to either scientifically sound or more inclusively generated policy: environment policy may thus have limited capacity to generate legitimacy for the EU through either output or input mechanisms.

Problems of EU environment policy

In addition to the problems of environmental policy-making as a process discussed immediately above, it is necessary to consider certain other difficulties facing the Union in its pursuit of environmental objectives: the implementation gap, enlargement, subsidiarity, mainstreaming, and new debates about policy mix/style.

The implementation deficit in EU environment policy has long been established (Collins and Earnshaw 1993). Domestic legislation made to enshrine agreements made at EU level does not always correspond to what EU actors considered had been agreed, in some cases because, given the emphasis on mainstreaming environment policy, EU legislation requires complex and difficult changes in different areas of domestic policy which are genuinely awkward to synchronise. In some cases, however, there is a less honourable reason: the wish to save money. Environmental legislation often imposes financial costs of a significant nature, which member states sometimes choose not to bear in practice even though they accept them in principle: there is no EU inspectorate able to ensure that member states comply with Union environmental policy, and many national governments are happy to take a gamble that the Commission will not seek their prosecution at the Court of Justice for non-compliance.[3] Sbragia (2000: 296) wryly notes that much of the most costly EU environmental policy was agreed in the 1970s, before the financial implications of such actions were fully appreciated by the member states.

Further enlargement of the EU will also provide difficulties. Past accession processes, including those to Spain, Portugal and Greece, have seen environmental protection sacrificed to market-making insofar as long-term derogations from environment policy were granted to candidate countries. The next round of enlargement, to countries of Central and Eastern Europe, is likely to produce similar sets of derogations; this can of course be justified as a case of equality between EU entrants of different accession rounds, but in terms of environmental protection it is likely to be problematic, especially given the worse condition of the environment in the countries of the former Soviet bloc than those of western Europe (Barnes and Barnes 1999).

Subsidiarity has caused problems for environment policy in that although there is acceptance at elite and popular levels that this is an area in which the Union should be active, member states appear to be increasingly watchful of the reach of EU environment policy into their domestic legislation, and may consider that this reach is now extensive enough. Fairbrass and Jordan (2001) show, for example, that EU biodiversity policy has significantly reduced UK autonomy in this issue area, and obliged it to adopt a different approach to policy-making from that which it had traditionally espoused. Although such influence is by no means automatic, because national systems can either resist or be incapable of responding to EU legislation (Knill 2001: 162–4), it certainly represents a similar example of EU ability to constrain member state freedom of manoeuvre to those, such as the supremacy of EC law, which member governments have been tenacious in contesting or even seeking to reverse (Taylor 1975; Weiler 1991).

Mainstreaming environment policy, a keystone of sustainability, has been problematic. The Treaty now enshrines sustainable development as a key goal of the Union. However, progress towards mainstreaming environment policy in other policy fields has been limited, partly because this requires complex, synchronistic policy-making, and partly because it requires all aspects of the EU institutions to give priority to environmental concerns. Empirical evidence (Warleigh 2000b) indicates that this cannot be taken for granted, and that within the Council, Commission and Parliament environmentalists must continually seek to make inter- and intra-institutional alliances in order to secure their objectives – with no guarantee of success.

Finally, the issue of policy mix/style has been important because the environmental field has often been considered to embody the Union's ability to provide positive integration (new collective policy) rather than regulation which seeks merely to remove barriers to trade. In fact, it has never been clear that EU environment policy owes more to 'positive integration' than to matters of the single market, because the latter has regularly been used as a reason for making environmental policy at Union level. However, the general shift in the EU towards 'soft policy' rather than the making of binding authoritative decisions does reduce the Union's ability to *demonstrate* its role as more than a market to the citizen. Moreover, it may reverse the traditional role of Union environment policy – the reinforcement, and even creation of national environmental legislation – by favouring those member states whose systems are best able to adapt to the 'soft policy' approach, rather than those which have a strong commitment to environmental protection (Knill 2001).[4] Thus, environment policy in the EU is subject to a number of challenges which indicate that past achievements may be its zenith.

Prospects for EU environment policy

One of the major problems of EU environment policy has been its need to mix a market-making/balancing rationale with one of ecology. Van der Straaten (1993) argues that the economic origins and justification for much legislation in this area undercut its effectiveness, because neoclassical economic reasoning rather than environmentalist thinking has been applied to it. Much EU policy regards environmental degradation as a 'negative externality' which has to be rectified by policy-makers; this view is problematic, because such corrective action requires not just political will but the ability to place a financial value on environmental degradation. The latter in particular can be difficult to achieve since environmental damage can be hard to quantify in orthodox financial terms, and thus the price paid for the addition of environment policy to the *acquis* has been acceptance of a limited approach to environmentalism. Although the principle of sustainability could go some way towards removing this problem, the limited progress made in implementing sustainable development in the EU to date denotes that there is yet to be a sufficient shift in values on the part of key social and political actors (Van der Straaten 1993: 81–2; Barnes and Barnes 1999: 5). A similar issue is the real but constrained progress on mainstreaming green issues within other policies; despite success in areas such as cohesion policy, it is not yet clear that either member states or the Union institutions so far take seriously their commitment to integrate environmental protection into all other policies. Indeed, given the emphasis placed in recent years on economic and monetary union, defence and immigration policies, it is possible that environment policy has become a second tier policy rather than a priority (Sbragia 2000).

Environmental protection remains controversial, however, at least as far as the manner in which it should be undertaken is concerned. The member states continue to differ acutely about the approach they advocate (Lévêque 1996c); this ongoing disputation adds to the recent general shift in EU decision-making towards soft policy to render the policy regime highly complex and not necessarily more effective. For example, implementation of environment policy continues to be imperfect: the shift towards 'soft policy' has not so far improved member state will to apply the legislation to which they have agreed despite giving them maximum discretion over how this should be done.

Furthermore, it may be that the Union's ability to use environment policy to develop its role as an international actor is reaching its limits. There is no doubt that the Union has been able to shape many international agreements in a way which reflects a deeper commitment to environmentalism than would otherwise have been the case (Sbragia 2000), and this success is laudable. However, as Zito (2000) points out, the Union's ability to shape global environment policy often ultimately rests on its ability to deny non-EU actors access to the single market. Viewed positively, this means the EU has significant leverage over those actors who wish to trade in the Union, and can impose environmental regulations as a condition of market access. Viewed negatively, this means that the Union's role as a single market is again privileged, and that environmentalism is not advanced for its own sake; this matters because sustainability requires not just political will (which can be generated through compulsion) but the application of different values (which are less easy to impose). The neo-liberal orientation of the WTO indicates that such value change is still far off: the recent débâcle over the Kyoto accords on climate change illustrates both the necessity for global action and the difficulty in securing it in the face of resistance from the only remaining superpower, the USA.

There is another significant challenge to Union competence in international environment policy, however, which may ultimately be more telling. Ironically, the logic which justifies Union action on environmental issues – the transfrontier nature of pollution, the need to protect common resources, the wish of activists to escape national systems which offer few possibilities for effective action – can equally be applied to the global level of governance. Interest groups seeking to secure ecological objectives employ 'forum shopping' to ensure they secure maximum advantage (Kellow and Zito 2002); the advantages gained by the Union in the past through its ability to provide an alternative policy-making arena to what may be rather closed national systems will now have to be shared with the emerging global level of governance. To this extent, the Union may simultaneously have to confront real limits to its ability to act at the global level. It may also have to face a reduction of its ability to capitalise on the will of many activists to work beyond and through the member states at a trans- or international level, given the existence of competing actors and regimes 'above' the national level (Warleigh 2001c: 632).

Consequently, and in sum, the prospects for environment policy in the Union are mixed. A substantial body of legislation has been built up, in some cases without an explicit legal base, indicating that the Union is capable of creative response to changing policy needs. The EP and other non-state actors have certainly played a key role in shaping much of the relevant *acquis*, complementing the growth of Union capacity in this issue area and its acquisition of flagship status as an example of 'positive integration' – that is, the creation of new common policies rather than the eradication of barriers to trade. These factors indicate that environment policy will continue to play an important role in the developing European Union. However, the increasing challenge of internationalisation (as opposed to Europeanisation) in this policy area presents the Union with great difficulties in terms of adapting policy style and content (Sbragia 2000). In addition, this shift could also undermine the EU's ability to present itself as a logical focus for those citizens seeking to be, in the phrase of Keck and Sikkink (1998) activists beyond borders. Sustainability is an important principle and has been enshrined in the Treaty; however, real progress towards its implementation has been slow. Therefore, the prospects for EU environment policy are mixed, and its ability to generate either output or input legitimacy for the Union cannot be taken for granted. It is now apposite to examine whether an analysis of Union regional policy generates a substantively different view.

Regional policy: origins and principles

The development of regional policy competence by the European Union in the 1970s has an innovative quality, in that it marks the Union out as a transnational polity with a clear redistributive function. No other international organisation has this power; although the UN, for example, is active in terms of foreign development policy aimed at countries in the 'third world', transferring money from 'North' to 'South', only the EU has any kind of explicit financial redistribution between its member states, none of which are below global poverty levels, justified by reference to the need for reduction of economic disparities between them. Regional policy is thus a tool for the more harmonious economic development of the Union. It is also, at least potentially, a device to harness, or even generate, cross-border solidarity between member state nationals, based on the idea that in the single market context all citizens benefit from helping lagging regions to develop economically.

A confluence of three factors pushed the Union in this direction. First, the longstanding drive for monetary union, which was relaunched by the Werner Report of 1970, and considered to require a redistributive mechanism to give the currency regime credibility; the accession to the Union of the UK, Ireland and Denmark in 1973, which increased the number of underdeveloped regions in the Union significantly; and the need to compensate for the restrictions to state aids required by EU competition policy, which made regional development more difficult (Bache 1998, 1999). Thus, regional policy has a place as part of the 'European model' of economic development, which tends to be less aggressively laissez-faire than its US counterpart, privileging instead the Keynesian idea of regulated capitalism (Loughlin 1997: 441–2; Hooghe 1998). Indeed, as a result of the Treaty on European Union, the EU has dedicated itself to the principle of 'economic and social cohesion' – that is, to improving the socio-economic equality between its richer and poorer regions (De Rynck and McAleavey 2001). However, behind this conjoined set of pressures lay another rationale: the idea of the 'juste retour' (fair return) on EU membership, which became interpreted in more crudely financial terms upon UK accession. With a great number of underdeveloped regions and a high contribution to the EU budget that was not made good by receipts under the CAP, the UK sought to make sure that membership of the Union was not a financial burden in direct terms – eventual participation in the single market would bring real, but less immediately quantifiable or visible, financial benefits (Dinan 1999: 431). So, as Thielemann (2002) argues, there is a strong 'compensation logic' in evidence at the heart of regional policy, which has often overshadowed its impact on regional development – especially as all member states continue to wish to be seen to benefit from it (Marks 1996: 390–1; Keating and Hooghe 2001).

Union regional policy is split into two main categories: *structural funds* (the European Regional Development Fund; the European Social Fund; the Financial Instrument for Fisheries Guidance; the Guidance Section of the European Agricultural Guidance and Guarantee Fund), and the *cohesion fund*. The cohesion fund has a much smaller budget, and is targeted at the improvement of environmental and transport infrastructures in Spain, Greece, Ireland and Portugal. For the period 2000–6, the Union has three priorities, and a total regional policy budget of € 213 billion (divided into € 195 billion for structural funds, and € 18 billion for the cohesion funds).[5] The three priorities are to fund EU regions whose economic development is lagging (Objective 1); to assist infrastructure development in areas with significant structural problems (Objective 2); and to fund training and job creation in areas not eligible for funding under Objective 1 (Objective 3). There are also programmes called Community Initiatives, which account for 5.35% of the structural funds. These Initiatives target cross-border, bottom-up projects on improving regional cooperation, rural development, and anti-discrimination measures in the marketplace. Finally, there is a programme dedicated to similar objectives as the cohesion funds, but aimed at countries seeking accession to the Union – ISPA (the Instrument for Structural Policies for Pre-Accession).

The principles of regional policy are *additionality* (the EU requires member states to co-fund projects it finances, instead of using structural/cohesion funds as a means to avoid making a financial contribution to regional development); *partnership* (the idea that local/regional actors, both elected and from the voluntary and private sectors, should work jointly with the Commission and national governments to devise and implement regional policy); *programming* (the refusal to fund ad hoc projects, and the decision instead to favour those which are part of a coherent overall development plan); and *concentration* (the targeting of certain agreed objectives, in an attempt to maximise results) (Hix 1999: 257). Taken together, these principles give regional policy a solid basis and also lend the Union the ability to be proactive, rather than remedial, in its redistributive policy actions (Loughlin 1997). They also enable the EU directly to 'penetrate ... the politics and society of the individual member states' (Hooghe 1996a: 5), because the Commission and non-state actors have an unusually significant formal role in the design and execution of the policy (Hooghe 1996a: 6–7).

The impact of regional policy: legitimacy
through redistribution and inclusion?[6]

However, there is significant doubt that EU regional policy has been able to contribute to the reduction of inequalities between regions of the member states in a meaningful way – and not just because the finance allocated for this purpose is relatively small, if growing as a proportion of the EU budget, or because the policy has sought to improve regional 'economic functionality' rather than social equality per se (Hooghe 1998: 459). Doubtless, many projects funded by the Union have had a positive impact on their locales; however, there is little evidence that funding decisions have been made according to objective economic assessments, but rather according to the compensation logic discussed above (Pollack 1995; Allen 2000). Consequently, much of the funding has been allocated according to the lobbying successes and veto threats of the central governments of the member states, rather than the demonstrable needs of their regions; moreover, the additionality principle has frequently been breached, often leading to the retention by central governments of money destined by the Union for regional development, and eventually causing the formal dilution of the additionality principle (Bache 1998, Chapter 6). EU regional policy has clearly supported, rather than replaced, national policies of this kind (Conzelmann 1998). So, despite the fact that there has been a significant transfer of resources from net contributor member states to those which are net recipients (Hix 1999: 260) this has not yet equated to a significant reduction in regional disparities.

Nonetheless, to some extent regional policy may contribute to the EU's legitimacy by means of a *logic of inclusion* much of what it lacks in a substantive logic of redistribution. There is ample evidence that at least some local and regional government actors have to some extent been able to use the opportunities presented by European integration, such as the creation of the Committee of the Regions, to increase their influence over EU policy (Bomberg and Peterson 1998; Tömmel 1998; Warleigh 1999). Given the legislative weakness of this Committee, however, a crucial variable here is often taken to be the ability of such actors to exploit opportunities afforded them by national constitutions: those from federal states have tended to be more influential in EU policy making, either directly or via national channels, than those from states with weak local or regional government structures (Marks 1996; Jeffery 2000).[7] The innovative partnership principle, created in the 1988 reform of the structural funds, and reformed in 1993 to reach beyond regional/local government actors to civil society groups, has great potential significance in this regard, however. This is because partnership may compensate actors with weak institutional status in the government structure of the member states (or none at all, in the case of the voluntary sector and social partners) by making them part of the networks which collectively create EU policy (De Rynck and McAleavey 2001). Regional level actors can, and sometimes do, use EU policy-making as an opportunity to make new alliances, both domestically and transnationally, in order to outmanoeuvre domestic opposition to their objectives in either the public or the private sector (Conzelmann 1998; Thielemann 2002). At the very least, partnerships can stimulate interest in, and awareness of, the impact of EU policy in a given region (Hooghe 1998). Thus, institutional weakness may not rule out the capacity to influence, and new forms of collaborative regional policy governance by partnership across EU, national and sub-state levels could arise in cases where sub-state actors are willing and able to mobilise the relevant resources and expertise (Tömmel 1998: 55).

And yet, it is not clear that the partnership principle has, in general, provided a new form of governance which can socialise public and private actors from the local/regional level into EU policy-making and allow them significant influence over policy outcomes (Thielemann 2000). According to Hooghe (1998), most regional policy partnerships have prioritised economic efficiency rather than substantive democracy or solidarity between members. Moreover, both Jeffery (2000) and Thielemann (2000) have shown that sub-state government actors do not necessarily bring strong democratic credentials to the decision-making process; for Jeffery, those without the backing of a vibrant civil society are unlikely to be able to add legitimacy, as opposed to efficiency, to the decision-making process via their presence in the relevant networks. For Thielemann, sub-state government actors can actually seek to exclude civil society groups from partnerships, using the latter to secure their own objectives but paying scant credence to the issues of democratic inclusion on which partnerships are supposed to be based. Tömmel (1998: 65–7) relates similar reservations. Thus, the real capacity of partnerships to increase Union legitimacy is at best open to question, especially when it is considered that in practice many partnerships suffer from unclear procedures and division of responsibilities, and tend to rely on existing structures and processes of governance rather than bottom-up innovation in governance practice (Hooghe 1998). Furthermore, there is often a conflict of interests between the actors involved in partnerships, which results in a constant need to resolve tensions rather than a new common interest (Tömmel 1998: 58). The question of central government gatekeeping also remains crucial. For many authors (Bache 1998, 1999; Allen 2000; Bache and Jones 2000; Sutcliffe 2000; Keating and Hooghe 2001) national governments retain (or have reclaimed) the key function in deciding how partnerships work, and who is allowed to be part of them. Indeed, the latest round of regional policy reform in 1999 limited the Commission's influence, and returned control of the partnership process to national governments (Keating and Hooghe 2001: 249–50). Consequently, although new partnerships and roles for both sub-state governments and civil society actors have been created as a result of EU regional policy, and certainly such actors have participated more regularly in EU decision-making as a result, it is far from clear that they are regularly able to wield significant *influence* over policy outcomes (Bache 1999). It appears that the undoubted potential of the partnership principle to reconfigure approaches to power-sharing and legitimacy-generation in the EU has yet to be realised: indeed, it may well be that the member states have deliberately frustrated it in order to retain control of a policy which might otherwise lead to increased budget contributions, or a loss of receipts from the structural/cohesion funds, after further EU enlargement to countries which all have a better a priori claim to such funding than its current recipients (Allen 2000).

Prospects for EU regional policy

The prospects for radical reform of Union regional policy are small. Current thinking in the national governments of the member states appears to favour budgetary rigour rather than Keynesian projects involving significant public spending, as set out in the Stability and Growth Pact regarding the single currency. It is very unlikely that any current member state will agree to pay substantially more for their EU membership in terms of contributions to the Union budget than they presently do (Allen 2000). Indeed, there has been a recent trend in several member states to demand 'their money back', following the lead of former UK Prime Minister Margaret Thatcher. Given this climate, and the continuing political imperative to ensure that all member states, rather than those regions in most need, receive something from the regional policy budget,[8] it is almost impossible to envisage a fundamental rethinking of EU regional policy which can improve the EU's legitimacy from either input (partnership) or output (significantly reduced regional economic disparities) perspectives. For certain scholars, there has always been a tension between the economic and social goals of EU regional policy, which, although never officially resolved, appears over time to have favoured the former given the Union's tendency to privilege economic rather than political integration and its consequently limited capacity to squeeze flanking policies out of the single market legislation (Behrens and Smyrl 1999; De Rynck and McAleavey 2001; Thielemann 2002).

The principles of EU regional policy – particularly additionality and partnership, but also programming and concentration – have been undermined, primarily through a lack of sustained member state commitment to the necessary structural and budgetary changes. Additionality has often proved an aspiration rather than an injunction, given member state capacities to retain EU funds at the centre (Keating and Hooghe 2001). Partnership has similarly failed to be implemented as intended when it was created in 1988. Even the Commission White Paper on European

Governance expresses reduced ambitions for the principle, making a brief mention of partnership in the context of 'more effective and transparent consultation' (CEC 2001: 15–17). Of course, consultation is not the equivalent of participation in policy formation as an equal partner (Sloat 2002) and it is not clear whether the Commission's wish to extend partnerships to 'certain sectors' (CEC 2001: 17) refers to either *policy* sectors or sectors of the *community*, or both. Thus, the partnership principle remains at something of a low ebb. Given the political imperative to ensure each member state receives something from the regional policy budget, neither programmatic planning nor efficient concentration of resources have been possible. As a consequence, EU regional policy has disappointed both advocates of regional development and those who saw it as an instrument by which the Union could demonstrate its utility to the citizen and facilitate popular engagement with the integration process.

Conclusions

The argument of this chapter has been that significant EU action in environmental and regional policies has not been able to impede the perception of the Union's 'democratic deficit' despite the fact that citizens consistently appear to view EU competence in these areas as legitimate. Of course, it is possible that such considerations can be outweighed by citizens' concerns about EU activity in policy areas they consider outside its appropriate scope, or its inability to intervene in areas they consider its natural preserve (see Blondel et al. 1998). It is also possible that different EU policies with a high profile, such as defence (the Rapid Reaction Force) or the single currency may in time provide evidence that the acquisition of competence can improve the Union's perceived legitimacy. However, in this chapter I have demonstrated that such consequences of competence acquisition cannot be taken for granted, because the EU must be able to deliver in practice what it promises in the Treaty. Here, the evidence points towards policy shortfalls, albeit by no means complete failure, in the two policy areas discussed. Environmental policy faces significant problems of non-implementation, and is also undergoing a change from hard regulation to soft policy which arguably reduces its capacity to improve the conditions of the European environment. Moreover, much of the justification for EU action in environment policy – the truism that pollution knows no frontiers – can also be applied to the more broadly international arena, and at this level the EU often faces difficulties in securing strong policy agreements between itself and non-member states. Regional policy remains relatively underfunded. Thus, the Union's ability to reduce regional disparities is rather limited. Furthermore, there is a mounting body of evidence that the local- and regional-level partnerships which are supposed to play a key role in the making of regional policy remain under the control of central governments, thereby frustrating their potential to create opportunities for participation and socialization into the EU system.

This conclusion points to the ability and will of member governments to restrict the democratic development of the EU when they consider (sometimes incorrectly) that such developments require either an inevitable sacrifice of national sovereignty, a change of policy paradigm, or unreasonable contributions to the EU budget (Warleigh 2002b). In the next chapter, I ask whether the same influence can be observed in the process of demos-formation, perhaps the principal democratic challenge of the EU.

NOTES

1 For an excellent overview of EU environment policy and its various instruments, see Barnes and Barnes 1999, Chapter 2.

2 Of course, EU decision-making is not reducible to a crude stand-off between national governments on one side and the EU institutions and interest groups on the other. Indeed, without making partners of at least key member states, other actors are unlikely to have any influence at all, and member states often have an incentive to seek such partnerships in order to overcome problems with their peers in Council. I suggest here merely that where non-state actors fail to act in coalition with a suitable number of member states they are likely to be frustrated in their attempts to influence policy.

3 The Court has the ability to fine member states for non-compliance, but neither environmental groups nor individual citizens have the right to take national governments to the ECJ. Instead, they must persuade the Commission to do so, and the Commission does not always consider such action politic.

4 Of course, such 'soft policy' may be more legitimate than 'hard policy' if it reflects conscious member government choices backed up by public opinion. However, it obviously questions the Union's ability to generate perceived legitimacy by means of producing detailed, binding legislation.

5 See www.europa.eu.int/comm/regional_policy/intro/regions2_en.htm

6 The demos-formation aspects of this issue are discussed in Chapter 6, and are not addressed here.

7 Moreover, as Jeffery (2000) also points out, it cannot automatically be assumed that actors from the sub-state level will always be supportive of European integration. Indeed, the case of the German Länder indicates that the reverse may be true (see also Devuyst 1998).

8 Witness the demands of the Spanish government at the Nice Summit of December 2000. Such thinking is also common to the wider regional policy community, albeit in many cases as a strategic rather than a normative conviction (see the 'compte-rendu' of the Second European Forum on Cohesion, Brussels, 21–22 May 2001: www.inforegio.cec.eu.int/tempomm/document/synthe_fr.pdf).

6

Demos Construction:
The Arrested Development
of European Citizenship

The absence of a European 'demos', that is, a 'community of citizens linked to each other by strong democratic bonds and pressing to acquire a measure of effective control through formal or informal means over government' (Chryssochoou 1998: 89) is the principal problem faced by the architects of democratisation in the EU. As Lord argues, institutional innovations can go only so far in removing perceptions of a democratic deficit in EU politics; without 'a shared identity, a common deliberative forum, and an open system of communications' (1998a: 132), citizens are unlikely to be aware of whatever institutional change is effectuated. Even if there is no such awareness problem, citizens are also unlikely to translate such institutional change into a more positive view of the Union without first having a deeper positive evaluation of two crucial variables. First, citizens must consider that they belong together with people of a different member state nationality as part of the same political community. Second, they must feel that the system itself is legitimate because it is one with which they can engage and which broadly reflects their identity and values, so that disaffection about a particular issue or policy does not semi-automatically become disengagement with the system as a whole.

By and large, the political systems of the member states enjoy this luxury: citizens may be disaffected with politics or with (particular) politicians, but this does not usually translate itself into either criticism of the very idea of the member state or a desire to withdraw from the national political community on the grounds that its members do not have sufficient shared values and practices (separatist movements of stateless nations such as the Basques notwithstanding). The EU does not have such a resource on which to draw.[1] Thus, when popular criticism of the Union is voiced, the perceived acceptability of the system as a whole is likely to be further undermined. For example, the EP's role in the resignation of the Santer Commission did not translate into greater public involvement with Parliament, or even greater turn-out in the EP elections which followed shortly after the Commission resignation. In fact, the turn-out *fell*: citizens appear either to have been unable to differentiate between the two institutions sufficiently or to have considered that the downfall of the Commission was yet further indication of the inherently unsatisfactory nature of the Union political system. So, while there is neither the need for the EU to develop an ethnically-defined sense of identity akin to that of its member states, nor any reason to conclude that this precludes the Union from developing a sufficient, if novel, sense of demos (Weiler et al. 1995), it is clear that the issue of how to engender a sense of shared values and political practice is in need of urgent attention.

In this chapter I begin by setting out both the normative and the strategic reasons for which demos-formation has become so vital to the Union's democratisation. I then proceed to examine the concept of 'demos', and consider its links to ideas of 'citizenship' and 'nation'. Having defined 'demos' as a civic, political identity based on shared values and practices, I then examine the development to date of EU citizenship, which was formally created by the Maastricht Treaty. I ask whether this new kind of citizenship has been able to help engender a greater sense of demos either through its formal inclusion in the Treaty or through the inculcation of 'citizenship practice' (Wiener 1998) – a new culture of political engagement by EU citizens, both with their co-citizens in different member states and with the institutions of the Union. The theme of the chapter can be summed up in the form of a question: has citizenship practice by member state nationals facilitated their development of a greater sense of belonging to a European demos? My argument is that, at least to date, only a negative answer to this question is possible, because both the substance of European citizenship (the rights and duties it confers), and the political opportunity structures available to citizens who seek to use their rights or otherwise engage with the EU system, are insufficient. European citizenship has great potential, both normatively (as a model of citizenship beyond the nation state), and practically (as a tool for demos-formation). However, for precisely this reason, EU citizenship has been 'frozen' (Warleigh 2001b) by the member governments, which have yet collectively to decide whether and how far they really wish to proceed with the democratisation process.

The necessity of demos-creation: normative and strategic rationales

From a normative point of view, the necessity of demos-formation is fairly straightforward; indeed, it has already been highlighted above. However, it is worth going into more detail here in order to develop a rounded understanding of the matter. There are perhaps three principal issues to consider. First, the fact that both public support for the EU, and the levels of identification with it at popular level, are low. Second, the need to ensure the single market does not have a detrimental impact on citizens' rights. Third, the need to ensure that the great, and increasing, diversity of political cultures and traditions within the Union is managed successfully.

Scholars who study opinion poll data about the extent to which citizens identify with either the Union or with nationals of other member states have not found great evidence of substantial identify shifts towards Europeanisation. Duchesne and Frognier (1995), for example, carried out a very thorough analysis, in which they conceived identity as capable of multiple expressions at any one time – that is, they considered it possible for individuals to hold multiple identities rather than one identity which excludes all other forms of membership, solidarity or sense of belonging together. Even so, they found that there was little evidence in any member state that its nationals had begun to identify either with the EU or with their counterparts in the other member states. Indeed, in some member states (the Netherlands, France and Germany), Duchesne and Frognier observed a strong trend in the opposite direction. Perhaps their key finding, however, was that even citizens who expressed a positive view of either the integration process in general or particular aspects of the Union did not automatically therefore identify more closely with the Union or nationals of other member states. Thus, even citizens who perceive value in European integration are not necessarily possessed of a sense of belonging together in a common political system with nationals of other member states; indeed, the process of deepening political integration at EU level appeared to be reinforcing popular attachment to national identities (Duchesne and Frognier 1995: 198–201).

Everts and Sinnott (1995) also found that although strong public support for internationalisation (or Europeanisation) of some policy issues can be perceived, this by no means equates to a strong sense of support for, or identification with, the EU as a whole – partly because the EU's actual policy competences do not accurately reflect those which the public considers appropriate (see also Blondel et al. 1998), and partly because support for the EU tends to be superficial rather than based on either accurate knowledge or experience. Gabel (1998b) argues that we can understand this superficiality further by remembering that the EU has been obliged to generate its legitimacy primarily by producing public goods. This has meant that most citizens either support or disfavour the EU according to utilitarian analyses based on cost-benefit calculations, if they have any opinion at all. For every policy decision taken, the EU may please some actors, but it will displease others, and those in both pro- and anti-EU camps change according to the issue in question. Thus, although the EU must clearly produce policy outcomes which most citizens generally consider worthwhile, it cannot rely on this 'output legitimacy' (see Chapter 1) to generate either a deeper sense of loyalty to itself, or cross-border solidarity.

This problem becomes more acute when the fact that the single European market relies ultimately on freedom of labour movement, as well as that of capital, goods and services, is remembered. Individuals seeking to breathe life into the single market by moving to another EU country pose a normative challenge to the Union in two ways. First, they must not be penalised for so doing by the loss of rights and entitlements which they would otherwise enjoy (e.g. the right to social protection). Second, they oblige, by their very movement and resettling, the citizens of their new domicile state to accept that former 'aliens' now share equal status with them 'in their quality as citizens of the Union' (Everson and Preuss 1995: 30). Therefore the EU cannot content itself with legitimacy-generation through the mere production of suitable public goods, because the integration process has developed to the point at which the Union is capable of having a negative impact on the rights of member state nationals: instead, the Union must actively ensure that member state nationals can benefit anywhere in the EU from an agreed minimum of rights, and that, in the form of a new social contract, efforts are made to encourage mutual recognition by member state nationals as fellow inhabitants of a European political space (Closa 1996).

The third normative reason for demos-formation is the need to ensure that the diversity of the Union in terms of (sub-)national cultures and traditions is preserved, while simultaneously ensuring that these diverse cultures and traditions coexist successfully within a joint governance system. Without a sense of belonging to some greater whole, member state nationals are unlikely to perceive either anything significant in common with nationals of other member states, or a reason why they should coexist in a common political system. This issue is thrown into sharp focus by the prospect of further EU enlargement, although it has always been present. The EU is due to take in 10 new states in 2004. This raises fundamental normative issues for the Union, because citizenship relies on a sense of exclusion – only citizens can be full members of a given polity, and citizens are often defined negatively, i.e. by comparison with 'other' groups whose characteristics, values or traditions they do not share (see Chapter 1). With great irony, it has often been by contrast with Central and Eastern Europe that West European states have sought to define both what they share and what is 'European' (Hedetoft 1997); the fact that there are significant numbers of Muslims in many of the current candidate countries increases their 'Otherness' in the eyes of many, as pointed out by Modood (1997). And yet, it is in precisely these countries that any real value has been invested in the drive for a 'European' identity (Hedetoft 1997). Paradoxically, then, it is only with enlargement to Central and Eastern Europe that the EU can credibly claim to be 'European', as opposed to *West* European. However, this very enlargement poses significant challenges to the Union by its likely causation of exponential growth in EU diversity of tradition, culture and practice. Without a far greater sense of common political identity, this increased cultural diversity is likely to undermine EU legitimacy (Scharpf 1999).

These normative reasons for the creation of a Euro-demos sit alongside strategic rationales based on calculations of system need. Of course, it is misleading to argue that the two are entirely separable; indeed, in the creation of EU citizenship, both normative and strategic rationales are clearly evident, and the former have of course framed what actors considered suitable strategic behaviour. However, it is worth pausing here to consider how demos-creation might be *Realpolitik* as well as normatively desirable, since ideals are only partially able to explain political events. The issues to consider are institutional interests, and system preservation.

In terms of institutional interest, it should be noted that the Commission in particular has often been active in trying to encourage interest groups to engage with the EU policy-making process, in order to create 'supportive networks' (Héritier 1999) of actors which it can claim represent civil society, in order both to claim greater legitimacy for itself and to demonstrate that civil society can engage with it successfully. This is not to say that the Commission has always succeeded; indeed, as is made clear below, the development of EU citizenship to date can be interpreted in terms of a power struggle between actors in the Commission and the member states on the question of legitimising Union institutions (Magnette 1999). However, it does indicate that many EU actors have seen institutional interest to lie in developing at least some kind of nascent Euro-demos (Warleigh 2001c). Calculations of the requirements for system preservation provide a similar rationale for limited demos-creation. Actors unpersuaded by the normative arguments made above in connection with the impact of the single market were more favourably disposed to the need to ensure the single market worked in practice. In other words, certain member governments had no wish to give the EU any kind of substantive demos, but they did wish to ensure that the single market, in which they were set to invest a great deal of political and economic capital, would not fail as a result of insufficient freedom of movement. In this view, the decision to deepen the integration process required certain necessary flanking measures which simply had to be tolerated, in order to ensure that increased interdependence did not either make the Union unstable (Bauböck 1994) or impose too much centralism. In this sense, limited demos-creation at the EU level (through provisions on EU citizenship), was simply a continuance of the welfarist re-casting of the nation state at the end of the Second World War (Davidson 1997).

Constructing a transnational demos: citizenship
without nationhood for the European Union?

In the case of a transnational polity such as the European Union, demos-creation is likely to be a more contested and difficult process than that at national level for two main reasons. First, demos-creation in the EU has to take place against the backdrop of many existing demoi in the member states, rather than in a vacuum. It will not, therefore, be possible to develop a sense of 'Euro-demos' unless this can be done in such a manner as to allow the rearticulation, rather than the replacement, of existing senses of demos. Second, there is no hegemonic actor capable of imposing a new sense of demos to the exclusion of all others, as happened in the case of many nation states. Instead, this new sense of demos will have to develop through the cooperation and participation of those who will enact it – that is, the citizens – with institutional actors and structures providing a sup-portive framework (Closa 1998a, 1998b). As a consequence, demos-construction at the EU level requires recognition of 'national specificities', and so pluralism rather than majoritarianism is required (Dehousse 1995: 131); moreover, demos-construction requires recognition that the EU, which is a political system but not a (nation) state (Schmitter 2000) has no automatic state-building *telos*, and thus that both states and citizens are valid sources of Union legitimacy (Chryssochoou 1998: 67).

As a result, it is necessary to define 'demos' in civic, or political, rather than ethno-cultural terms. The objective of demos-formation in the EU is to find an effective, affective means by which citizens can recognise each other as co-citizens of a common political system, and also recognise the system itself as legitimate. It is *not* to create a totalising 'Euro-identity' which smothers those of the member states and their component regions, or which seeks to engender support for the formation of a Euro-state. A Euro-demos is thus not equivalent to a *nation*,[2] because it focuses on civic inclusion and shared values rather than common traditions, ethnic identities or cultures (Chryssochoou 1998: 89–98). Indeed, any 'European' demos would require the continued existence of the more organic (if still at least partially invented) cultures of the member states in order to give it the requisite resonance with citizens (Weiler 1995; Smith 1997).

It is for this reason that the creation of EU citizenship in the Maastricht Treaty is of such potential importance.[3] This Treaty gave member state nationals an extra citizenship, that of the Union. At a stroke, and formally speaking, it decoupled the ideas of nationality and citizenship, in that while EU citizenship is available only to member state nationals, it is also pre-sented explicitly in civic, rather than ethno-cultural, terms (Weiler et al. 1995: 20–24). The Treaty therefore pointed towards the possibility that citizenship could be reconfigured, and expressed simultaneously through transnational and national institutions and practices (Meehan 1993). Thus, it is necessary to examine the substance of EU citizenship, and the use to which it has been put, in order to establish whether and how it has been able to contribute to the development of a Euro-demos.

Formal treaty provisions on citizenship

EU policy on citizenship has evolved over time, turning from the provision of symbolic trappings of nationhood to the generation of greater opportunities for public participation in EU decision-making (Wiener 1998: 252). However, as Wiener (1998: 254) also notes, the Treaty provisions are clearly limited, constituting to a great extent a 'dusting-off' of existing parts of the *acquis* rather than substantive new rights. This is because, as for demos-formation more generally, both normative and utilitarian rationales lie behind the development of EU competence in citizenship: those member states and other actors seeking a means to make the Union more democratic were obliged to compromise with those seeking only the means to make the single market operationalisable (Warleigh 2001b: 21–3).

Although the Maastricht Treaty (and subsequent minor changes made at Amsterdam) do constitute a departure from the rather vaguer concept of a 'people's Europe', they do not represent a complete break with it (Magnette 1999). As an indicator here, it is worth recalling the work of the Adonnino Committee on a 'People's Europe'. Reporting in 1985, this committee made many proposals for the improvement of the EU's image and the deepening of a 'European' sense of identity. It also stated that the member states could do more to foster a sense of European political identity by actually implementing the policies to which they had already agreed (e.g. freedom of movement; a common electoral system for the European Parliament) than by florid rhetoric and symbols (Adonnino Committee 1985: 9–19). Some of the Committee's recommendations have since become EU policy (such as electoral rights for EU citizens living in a member state other than that whose nationality they possess, or the right to petition). However, many of them (not least legislation on freedom of movement) have still to be fully realised, despite progress; others, such as the creation of a peace corps to bring together young people from the different member states in order to work on social development projects, or the routine consultation by the member governments of citizens of their EU partner states about issues of domestic public policy, have yet to be realised at all.

The formal provisions on EU citizenship are to be found in articles 17–22 of the Treaty on European Union, as amended by the Treaty of Amsterdam. As noted already, these articles state that EU citizenship is automatically and solely available to member state nationals. There are no duties of EU citizenship. In terms of rights, the provisions include freedom of movement, the right to vote and stand in both local and EP elections in one's member state of residence rather than nationality, the right to diplomatic protection by other member states than one's own in third countries where one's own state has no official representation, the right to petition the newly-created Ombudsman and the European Parliament, and the right to write to EU bodies in any official EU language and receive an answer in the same language. These rights may be added to, but may not be reduced (Article 22). However, they are subject to opt-outs (e.g. voting rights can be denied under Article 19), and placed firmly within the power of the member governments to police. Thus, there is significant ambiguity about the extent and value of these rights as a means to develop a substantive form of EU citizenship, particularly given the role of member states as gatekeepers of citizenship (Kostakopoulou 2001: 77; Warleigh 2001b: 24–6; see O'Leary 1996 for a negative assessment, and Montani 1993 for a more positive evaluation). In addition, the Charter of Fundamental Rights, attached to the Nice Treaty, cannot (yet) add significantly to this list because the member states explicitly placed it outside the Treaty, meaning that its legal strength is at best questionable (Shaw 2001: 199). Thus, binding formal provisions on EU citizenship will remain less than extensive.

Citizenship practice

However, the limits of Articles 17–22 are not necessarily those of European Union citizenship; a case can be made that these limits impose constraints on engagement by citizens with the integration process, but they do not make it impossible. In fact, both the Treaties and secondary legislation give the citizen rights and entitlements which are not expressed in the formal citizenship provisions; the Court of Justice has also made judgments which appear to extend the scope of EU citizenship, even if it is mistaken to consider the Court as a necessarily teleological actor (Hunt 2001). Wiener (1996, 1998) has argued further, namely that citizenship must be considered as a 'practice' rather than simply a set of legal entitlements, and thus that it is what actors make of the limited Treaty provisions (and other legislation) which dictates the extent to which EU citizenship develops. For Wiener (1996: 46), citizenship practice is a mixture of formal rights (civil, social and political), access to the polity and public welfare provision, and a sense of belonging (understood as both practices such as tax-paying or participation in public debate, and legal ascriptions of nationality).

This broader view deserves consideration – and not just for the obvious reason that even the most extensive formal provisions on citizenship would have little impact on demos-formation if they failed to be routinely enacted by their beneficiaries. As Closa (2001) points out, without popular engagement with, and critique of, both national and EU claims to legitimacy, a deeper sense of the latter is unlikely to emerge. This is because the EU has no 'organic, mythical foundation' (Obradovic 1996: 191); and although Koslowski (1998) is right to argue that such a myth is not necessary because the Union is not trying to construct a nation, the Union clearly requires some other means to generate in its citizens a sense of belonging together. There is clear normative value in developing popular agency here, because, as Weale (1997: 136) points out, appropriate political behaviour ('cooperative practices') can shape political identity. Thus, individual citizens can shape their sense of political identity as they choose, at least to some extent, by entering and possibly re-shaping the political arena constructed for them by elites. If undertaken as a conscious project of active citizenship, this can generate a sense of 'constitutional patriotism' (Habermas 1996: 133), through which nationals of the different member states view political engagement with both each other and the EU system as the means by which it can provide both peaceful coexistence and the preservation of different cultural identities. It remains to investigate the extent to which individuals and groups have been able to realise the potential of citizenship practice in the European Union.

Realising citizenship practice?

The principal obstacle to be overcome by those seeking to realise citizenship practice in the EU is the fact that there are relatively few means by which individuals can contribute directly to EU decision-making. Although Nenwtich argues that there are many and increasing political opportunity structures available to EU citizens keen to engage with Union politics, he concludes that most of these methods are both informal and limited in their likely impact (Nentwich 1998). This is likely to remain the case in the medium term, as in order to engage properly with the Union actors from civil society require the EU to make further progress on openness and transparency than it has so far been able to manage (Bunyan 1999). Thus, individual citizens are far less likely to be able to engage with the EU and its politics than interest groups and non-governmental organisations (NGOs), whose relatively high profile and perceived legitimacy with the public may provide a means to attract citizens into the EU arena more effectively than either national governments or EU actors can manage, given that both the latter actor sets suffer from a poor public image which makes them unlikely to succeed as advocates of active citizenship in the Union context. Here, there are two potential barriers. First, are NGOs[4] and public interest groups able to lobby effectively in the EU, or are private interest groups able to monopolise successful lobbying? Second, can NGOs and similar organisations really help socialise citizens into the system, or do they rather represent a means by which citizens abdicate responsibility for active citizenship, and leave responsibility for political engagement with NGO staff?

On the first question, there seems little doubt that a positive answer is possible. Much empirical work indicates that although private interest groups are often better resourced and more able to develop partnerships with actors at both EU and national level to influence Union policy (Balanyá et al. 2000) NGOs certainly can lobby effectively and influence policy decisions made by the EU (for empirical evidence and a brief literature overview, see Warleigh 2000b). Such influence is not automatic, but it is often present, meaning that citizens who seek to influence EU policy via this means have at least some likelihood of success – if, that is, the second barrier (the ability of NGOs to socialise citizens into the EU system) is also surmountable.

Here, the evidence leaves little ground for optimism. As I argue elsewhere (Warleigh 2001c, 629–35), empirical investigations reveal that there are significant hindrances to NGOs' ability to socialise citizens into the EU system, as assessed against such criteria as financial independence, internal democracy, and political education. Although it would be misleading to argue that all NGOs fail to demonstrate any such capacity, it also appears that necessary structures to allow NGOs an EU-socialisation function, such as the existence of methods of internal decision-making which allow supporter input into NGO EU-strategy, are in general conspicuous by their absence. So too are mechanisms by which NGO supporters or members can hold these organisations to account, or make an input into their decision-making. Furthermore, it even appears that citizens are content that this should be the case. They appear to wish to delegate responsibility to organisations whose broad aims they support even if they are ignorant of, and might conceivably oppose, these organisations' policy stances on a range of issues. In sum, NGOs' ability to develop EU citizenship is thus very limited, at least for the time being. Usually able to maintain financial independence, and helpfully concentrating on advocacy and campaign work, NGOs which seek to influence EU policy nonetheless generally fail to provide the mechanisms by which supporters can equip themselves with the skills, knowledge and interests to become EU citizens in a substantive sense. Particularly telling are the shortfalls in structures of decision-making, internal democracy and supporter education; judged against these three crucial criteria, NGOs fall far short of the mark. For the time being, in this regard at least, NGOs engaging with the EU decision-making process are interest groups like any other and no more likely to provide a socialisation function than the private interest groups whose utilitarian, instrumental rationale for EU engagement they must share to operate effectively in the EU system (Warleigh 2000b).

Conclusions: Europe's 'should-be' demos

In a sense, this should be no surprise. As Schlesinger and Kevin point out, 'the contemporary political public sphere is peopled by groups organized in the pursuit of sectional interest rather than individual citizens intent upon discussing the common good' (2000: 207). However, this similarity between national and transnational contexts is of limited consolation to those seeking the development of a Euro-demos, because in national contexts such sector-specific, elite-led activism is anchored in at least some degree of perceived polity-belonging, whereas in the EU context this activism is the means by which such a sense of belonging is supposed to be generated. Without further means of development, there is little chance that active EU citizenship will evolve significantly as a practice to make good its formal shortcomings. Indeed, if sectoral groups continue to make claims in the name of EU citizenship at the instigation of actors in the Union institutions, they may well make the concept incoherent – sectional interests are by no means automatically in the general public interest (Magnette 1999).

An issue of crucial relevance here is the relationship between civil society actors and EU institutions. The White Paper on EU Governance (CEC 2001) indicates that a more substantial attempt to reach out to civil society groups than in the past may now be made. However, it is not yet clear whether these links will amount to acceptance of critical interchange or merely reconfigure the 'supportive networks' identified by Héritier (1999) in order cynically to reflect changing requirements about whose consultation is seen to be a possible source of legitimacy. The fact that there are no civil society representatives as such in the membership of the post-Nice Convention indicates that there is still some way to go.

Thus, it must be concluded that, at least so far, EU citizenship has not led to the establishment of a meaningful Euro-demos, as opposed to the single electorate created formally by Treaty provisions on the franchise for EP elections. Defined politically and civically, and distinguished from the concept of the 'nation', a demos nonetheless rests on a broad and widespread sense among its constituent individuals that they belong together insofar as joint action is taken to be necessary for problem-solving, and that in turn this provides the basis for a common political identity, albeit a multi-layered and evolving one. In the EU, there is little indication that citizens are of this opinion; indeed, it can be questioned whether citizens really want to play a more active role in EU governance, or just to express vague but increasing dissatisfaction with a Union that continues to be considered distant and arcane (Schmitter 2000: 18).

European Union citizenship is therefore a phenomenon with much potential that is withering on the vine for two reasons. First, in formal terms, it is underdeveloped, lacking both the duties which are necessary to cultivate a sense of mutual responsibility and many of the rights which might lend it greater salience. Second, in terms of citizenship practice, there are insufficient opportunities for political engagement, and a dearth of actors able to act as ambassadors for, or sponsors of, informed citizenship. These shortcomings can largely be attributed to the unwillingness of many member states to approve further reform. Bound by state-centric 'frames' of democracy and citizenship, both national governments and EU actors have tended to view the development of EU demos and an EU nation as synonymous (Kohler-Koch 2000; Warleigh 2002b). As a result, they have either opposed or sought the development of EU citizenship on the ground that it is a strategy for state-building, and their ongoing contestation has produced a set of citizenship rights and practices which are insufficient for the task at hand: enabling and encouraging citizens to play their full part in the process of democratising the Union. Over thirty years ago, Lindberg and Scheingold (1970) described the Union as a 'would-be polity'. After three decades of further integration, the EU's deepening as a political system has still to make member state nationals more than a 'should-be demos'. In the next, and final chapter, I address the issue of how this situation might be rectified.

NOTES

1   Cram (2001) argues that the EU does possess some ability to call on a sense of community held by EU citizens, in that the latter are used to its existence and grudgingly accept it as part of the political landscape, albeit one with which they are not happy. However, this 'banal Europeanism' does not equate to a sense of demos, as I make clear in this chapter.

2   For an overview of the formation of nations in Europe, see Hobsbawm (1997), Chapter 5.

3   For an extensive discussion of the reasons behind the creation of EU citizenship, see Warleigh (2001), Wiener (1998), Magnette (1999).

4   The term NGO can be fairly elastic. I here follow the definition of the World Bank (Operational Directive 14.70, 28 August 1989): NGOs are considered to be 'groups and institutions that are entirely independent of government and that have primarily humanitarian or cooperative rather than commercial objectives; they are private organisations that pursue activities to relieve suffering, provide basic social services, or undertake community development; they also include citizens' groups that raise awareness and influence policies'.

7

Conclusions: Towards Substantive Democracy in the European Union

The price of democracy in the European Union

In this final chapter I sum up the difficulties of the EU's democratisation project, drawing conclusions based on the studies of Union processes, structures and practices of governance contained in the previous chapters. I argue that although democratisation requires radical institutional change, to be effective it must be accompanied by the bottom-up formation of a greater sense of common political identity between EU citizens. Without such a shift, institutional revision is likely to be unperceived by the citizen, or considered irrelevant. Therefore, democratic reform of the Union must give priority to a process of *political socialisation* of member state nationals, both in general and about European integration in particular. Importantly, this process must be allowed to happen according to popular opinion, guided, but most definitely not dictated, by elites. In other words, in order to democratise the European Union we cannot afford either apathy or shibboleths: reform necessitates both being prepared to sacrifice the 'state-like' future so desired by federalists, which has not proved its worth, and facilitating popular engagement with the integration process, whose lack is ever more troubling. Thus, citizens also have to take ongoing responsibility for their own good governance, and entrench practices of active 'European' citizenship once the structures necessary to permit this have been put in place. The European Union, after all, is a means and not an end: it can serve a useful purpose in maximising public welfare, ensuring good governance in its member states and beyond, and keeping the peace of the continent, but only if it is considered a tool to be used in reaching these objectives, rather than their very essence. European integration is instrumental to the good governance of the member states; democracy must be inherent in it.

The irony of European integration may thus well be that those with the strongest attachment to the elitist 'Community Method' do the Union as great a disservice as those who cling resolutely to either the illusion of 'national sovereignty' as a normative idea or the 'beggar-my-neighbour' use of state power as governmental strategy.

The structure of the chapter is as follows. First, I summarise the main points of the first six chapters. Subsequently I re-visit the idea of the 'functional-ideational deficit' in order to re-establish what theories of EU democracy must take as their tasks and focus, and thereby set the conceptual frame for what follows. I then build my argument that EU democratisation is possible despite the Union's current difficulties if more successful strategies are elaborated to close the deficits of legitimacy and participation, and submit that democratic reform of the Union demands both the frank politicisation of the integration process and the further political socialisation of EU citizens. Finally, I set out some ideas for the democratic reform of the Union, moving towards a blueprint of EU governance which mixes norms, practices and institutions in a critical deliberativist manner.

The argument so far

In Chapter 1, I sought to define the 'democratic deficit' and explain how it has arisen. I argued that the real problems of EU democracy are substantive rather than formal, and relate principally to the absence of a meaningful Euro-demos (defined as a self-conscious body of citizens across the member states who consider the EU, and political engagement with both the Union and each other, as a natural course of action to be undertaken in order to secure their objectives). I argued that this deficit arose from the mistaken institutional design and developmental trajectory respectively given to and hoped for the Union by its key founders, who created technocratic structures that were supposed to create a federal state by stealth (and thus in the absence of popular engagement, or even knowledge). I set out the two main models of democracy in international politics, cosmopolitanism and communitarianism, and argued that neither can successfully be applied to the Union on its own. However, both schools of thought contain insights which can be helpful in reconsidering the democratic governance of the EU, given its existence at a changing point on the spectrums between national and international politics, and regional state and international regime.

Chapter 2 developed this argument further, focusing on exactly how the democratisation of the idiosyncratic EU system of the EU could be conceptualised. I maintained that the Union should be redesigned according to principles of what I call 'critical deliberativism', that is a deliberative theory of democracy which acknowledges the power of certain liberal democratic ideas and structures, chiefly on the issues of representation and adjudication. At the macro-level of system design, this model dictates a shift towards functionalism; at the micro-level, it dictates the development of a participatory system of governance which could in turn facilitate the emergence of a Europeanised civil society and citizenry. At both levels, a deeper acceptance of flexibility, gradualism, and experimentation is necessary in order to foster the change from formal to substantive democracy.

In Chapter 3, I examined the issue of how national sovereignty has been reconfigured in the EU, focusing on the principles of subsidiarity and flexibility. I argued that the extent to which the national autonomy of each member state has been voluntarily reduced by EU membership is significant. However, this reconfiguration is neither overt nor fixed, and has certainly been insufficiently advocated to the citizen. The member governments have generally been unwilling to engage in a proper debate at either elite or popular level about whether, and if so in what way, European integration is worth a 'sacrifice' of national sovereignty. Thus, subsidiarity and flexibility have so far largely been developed by both EU and national actors as managerial devices, not normative principles of governance. As a consequence, both subsidiarity and flexibility are conceptually underdeveloped, insufficiently elaborated, and unable to serve as a means by which sovereignty can be explicitly reconfigured in the EU context.

Chapter 4 focused on the issue of institutional reform, with particular reference to the EU body with both the most impressive evolutionary progress and the *prima facie* closest links to the citizen, namely the European Parliament. Here, I argued that the impressive gains in legislative influence achieved by the EP have not made either it or the Union more legitimate in the eyes of the citizen. This is partly because the EP still has few powers in many of the policy areas which surveys indicate citizens consider EU activity to be both appropriate and suitable for EP intervention (two variables which do not automatically coincide). However, and more importantly, it is also because the Parliament's new powers are exercised in a way which removes its legislative influence from the public gaze thanks to the requirements of the codecision process. As a consequence, the undoubted rise to influence of the EP reflects Union democratisation of a limited and formal, rather than substantive, nature.

In Chapter 5 I looked at whether the EU has been able to mirror the strategies of its member states in the period after the end of the Second World War by increasing its perceived legitimacy through the acquisition of increased competences and capacities in welfare provision. Studying two cases of EU policy competence which were both gained during the Union's evolution rather than at its outset and are both considered by citizens to be areas in which the Union can helpfully be active, environmental and regional policies, I argued that such a conclusion could not be drawn. This was for two principal reasons. First, the limited will of the member governments to commit sufficient finances to the EU system, thereby starving it of the resources necessary for a significant redistributive role and leaving much environmental policy to die of neglect as hollow words on the statute book. Second, the refusal of the member governments to commit to the principles of either policy: Treaty references to 'sustainability' have so far largely been empty, and 'partnership' is often, perhaps usually, a principle of policy-making which is honoured in the breach rather than the application. Therefore, and despite much EU legislation in these areas, the Union appears to be of limited utility to advocates of either ecologism or social democracy. Moreover, it is therefore difficult to justify the Union on the grounds that it is able to make a positive difference to many citizens' quality of life in anything but a narrowly economic way based on wealth-creation through membership of the single market.

In the penultimate chapter I examined the issue of whether, and how, member state nationals have been able to function as a demos, concentrating on the subject of EU citizenship. Here, I reached a similar conclusion. EU citizenship owes its existence to a dual rationale, based on making a success of the internal market and the creation of a direct link between the Union and the citizen. In its decade of life to date, however, the market-making element has dominated, and the Europeanisation of civil/civic society remains very limited. EU citizenship currently offers little to bind nationals of different member states together with each other, and inadequate opportunities to engage with the EU decision-making process. Thus, EU citizenship is somewhat frozen, a tool with much potential to help reduce the democratic deficit which is underdeveloped for precisely that reason.

Re-visiting the 'functional-ideational gap': structure, agency and substantive democracy in the EU

The common strand of all the chapters in this book – be they theoretical or empirical – is the observation that the member states have, at least so far, preferred to retain a very flawed EU system than to democratise it in any meaningful way. At best, some of the elements of a democratisation process have been assembled and imperfectly developed. At worst, the continuing fixation of national governments with the liberal democratic blueprint has made a majority of them fear Union democratisation as their own destruction by a new Euro-state of the Westphalian kind. Neither EU institutions nor citizens themselves have consistently sought to secure democratisation through other means than precisely this federal template, producing a 'lose-lose' situation.

As Lord (2001: 642) points out, making suggestions for democratic reform of the EU requires an understanding of two principal issues: first, the 'acquis démocratique' (i.e. the steps the EU has taken in order to improve its democratic credentials) and second, a normative blueprint capable of managing conflicts of *values* between citizens and governments. The first issue is discussed at length in Chapters 1–6. The second is particularly important to consider, given that, as pointed out in Chapters 1 and 2, not only European integration, but also democracy itself, are contested phenomena. As a result, any theory of EU democracy must take this contestation as a starting point from both normative and practical perspectives, and consider such debate healthy rather than symptomatic of either decline or lack of progress. Such contestation, after all, is both the essence of politics and the sign that something important – values, not simply policy preferences to be traded off against each other – is at stake.

Models of EU democratisation must also acknowledge that EU reform *should* be an ongoing process: by this I do not mean that gradual and piecemeal reform such as that we have so far witnessed is acceptable. Instead, I mean that the contestedness of both democracy and European integration dictates that there can be no once-and-for-all solution to the EU's democracy problems: popular preferences will legitimately differ over time, according to policy issue and in each of the member states. In turn, this points towards a difficult quadruple balancing act: between various (national elite) views of the purpose of the Union; between different levels of governance (European-national-regional-local); between output and input legitimacy; and between different normative views of democracy (Warleigh 2003). This balancing act must be made, and reviewed, repeatedly. The challenge for the EU, then, is to reform its governance structures and practices in order to allow for greater political participation by citizens, and thereby diffuse tension about the loss of *national* sovereignty through its evident replacement with *popular* sovereignty, articulated as a continuing process of self-governance and polity-design by a European demos (Linklater 1998).

Crucially, this means that radical institutional change, though clearly necessary, is only the first stage in the reform process. The EU cannot expect to develop a demos under its present institutional configuration; however, neither can it create one simply by changing its decision-making structures and institutions. Institutional change, such as the IGC due in 2004, can be only a first, facilitating stage in the process, undertaken to afford citizens the capacity to mobilise in the knowledge that such mobilisation will be influential. *Structure* is vital in shaping what actors can do, as 'new institutionalists' rightly remind us (see Warleigh 2001a). Indeed, as Zürn (2000) demonstrates, in transnational contexts such as the EU, institutions serve a crucial purpose as the means by which input legitimacy can be translated into output legitimacy. However, ultimately the vibrancy and nature of EU democracy will depend on what EU citizens do with, or to change, the structures they are given, i.e. their *agency*, which in turn may well influence the nature and role of the structures (Wendt 1987). Democratic reform of the EU should therefore be considered as an ongoing process, in which institutional change is informed by popular agency and in which evolution is taken as the only constant characteristic of governance structure. After all, the real constitution of a political system lies not so much in a legal text as in its social conditions, political culture and the opportunity structures and practices available to the citizen (Bellamy 1996, 2001; Wiener and della Salla 1997).

In this light, critical deliberativism offers a useful way forward. To reiterate an earlier set of claims (see Chapter 2), it can serve to set out how making decisions within each policy regime should be undertaken (so, even if each regime is configured differently in terms of institutions and processes, they may all work according to the same guiding principle). It can be a means by which policy regimes are created (through negotiation and mutual agreement to extend the EU's scope). It can serve as a means of adapting policy regimes/styles according to perceived need. Furthermore, it offers the means by which the EU can build further legitimate authority by enshrining the principle that all EU activity must be based on the explicit, voluntary compliance of those citizens it concerns. Most importantly, critical deliberativism seeks to generate, rather than assume the prior existence of, a sense of common interests and solidarity between EU citizens: on this basis, political action can be taken and justified, and communication between different communities and groups can be assured (Linklater 1998; Risse 2000).

However, again recalling Chapter 2, it should be remembered that critical deliberativism has a commitment to reflect upon its own suitability, accepting that the required form of deliberative democracy must both reflect the specific needs of the EU system and the limits to 'pure deliberation' which the latter imposes. Thus, 'critical deliberativism' is intended as a situation-specific conceptual framework which is open to the use of ideas from other traditions where this is both appropriate and conceptually coherent. To this end, it accepts that liberal democratic notions of representative democracy will have a role to play in ensuring, at least in the medium term, that citizens from different member states are able to communicate with each other in the absence of a common language. It also accepts that deliberation has limits, in that even the deepest form of input legitimacy is unlikely to justify the EU system if it is thereby paralysed and incapable of making important decisions.

Critical deliberativism and substantive democracy: back to functionalism for the EU

My purpose in this final section of the book is not to elaborate the details of how critical deliberativism might reshape the EU's political order and institutions, but rather to put forward some ideas about democratic reform of the EU based on a critical deliberativist application of some of the main tenets of functionalism. Elsewhere I have sketched out what a functionalist-inspired EU based on the principle of flexibility might require and provide in terms of system change and legitimacy respectively (Warleigh 2002a: Chapter 5). Therefore, I do not intend to repeat either that sketch or the detailed discussion of critical deliberativism contained in Chapter 2 of the present volume here.[1]

According to the leading functionalist, all public action is political (Mitrany 1975). Thus, all public action in the EU should be democratised. However, the key to this democratisation is a certain principle of fostered gradualism, in which ideational change, and so willingness to accept structural adaptation both regarding specific policy sectors and transnational cooperation in general, are facilitated by deliberate action by a 'vanguard' group of countries and citizens. Prematurely created common institutions would in all likelihood cause a backlash against the integration process; put simply, supranational institutions must arise from popular support for European integration, rather than attempt to create it. Functionalists considered that each policy sector should be governed transnationally by an agency accountable to a specialised assembly. Representative democracy would thus be reconfigured in favour of issue-specific patterns of citizen mobilisation and participation in/monitoring of these assemblies, rather than the general aggregation of interests across issues undertaken by political parties in liberal democracies. Given that not all citizens attach the same importance to all issues, and that nobody can possibly know enough about every issue in public life to have an informed opinion on all of them, citizens would be free to choose on which issues they care to mobilise. Functionalists consider that individuals – and states – are free to enter into a multiplicity of overlapping relationships, which serve to ensure that power is not overly concentrated in the hands of any one actor/group.

Functionalists consider *fixed* constitutions to be a device for the creation and preservation of a state structure (Mitrany 1965). Like all else in politics, constitutional arrangements should, in the functionalist view, *evolve*. However, this does not mean that functionalists consider that a written European constitution will emerge automatically if slowly. Legitimacy is seen by functionalists to derive from administrative capacity and legislative output, i.e. the maximisation of welfare (Mitrany 1975). Functionalists argue that supranational institutions must make no overt attempt to create a sense of loyalty to the emerging European order, because this is likely to cause offence and disquiet; instead, loyalty to the EU should emerge gradually and, because it arises from self-directed participation by citizens and states, it will suffer far less from a backlash than the currently-witnessed popular unrest about the future progress of the EU.

In terms of critical deliberativist views of EU democracy, functionalism has much to offer. It might be said to reflect at the level of international relations scholarship many of the concerns and perspectives of critical deliberativism within political theory. Its stress on sector-specific individual choice and participation is helpful, as is its insistence that European integration need not result in a state-like outcome. Its recognition of the value of some form of representative democracy, reworked to make it more meaningful to the citizen in the form of sectoral assemblies, is a good example of what critical deliberativism might advocate. As a normative theory, functionalism provides an explicit way to conceptualise European integration as a process of welfare-maximisation and peace-preservation, thereby returning citizens' focus to the core of the justification for the EU's existence. Furthermore, the functionalist expectation and acceptance of contestation over norms as well as policies is welcome, because it indicates that democratic governance cannot be secured in the EU as a result of elite-driven homogenisation or bargaining. Instead, functionalism relies upon consensus-formation, and accepts that in some cases such consensus may not be realisable. For functionalists, when consensus is absent, it is legitimate for those who can agree to do so and pursue collective action, while those whose agreement has not been given are free to abstain.

The consequence, of course, is the recognition that the EU may not have a federal future, or at least that it may not be able to extend this future to all its member states. Critical deliberativists accept such an outcome as normatively superior to state-building in the absence of popular consensus. They also support functionalism's argument that democratising the EU requires adopting a solid, explicit rationale for cooperation beyond borders, and its view that EU democracy requires a complex constellation of input and output legitimacy, structure and agency. Moreover, it shares functionalism's view that agency is ultimately more vital than structure, so long as the structure is suitably permissive for agency to occur. In addition, critical deliberativism accepts the functionalist focus on the acceptance of difference, particularly in the case of values. Thus, for both functionalists and critical deliberativists, it is vital to acknowledge that group and individual preferences rather than hierarchical divisions of power should be at the heart of EU governance, mediated by a culture of consensus through deliberation whose goal is to accept that different actors and groups will have legitimately different views about what the EU can, or should, do.

So, for critical deliberativists, the first, and crucial, step towards the democratisation of the EU is the adoption of a functionalist, rather than a federalist or state-centric 'frame' for the integration process. Within such a frame, norms and structures can be debated and revisited through an ongoing process of consensus-formation where possible, mediated by representative democracy where necessary. Thus, priority is given to a process of political socialisation through which member state nationals can re-invent themselves as 'European' citizens and thereby also shape the EU polity in the manner of their choosing, breathing life into subsidiarity and flexibility as guiding principles of EU governance. As the preceding chapters of this book have shown, isolated acts of constitution, or polity-building are unlikely to produce a substantive, rather than a formal, democratisation process: critical deliberativism would guarantee it.

However, this of course could pose further questions. If the EU is democratised substantively, will either national elites or EU actors be satisfied with the results? Will deliberation make the reform process even slower than it currently is? Is there, could there ever be, sufficient popular will to adopt the requisite forms of active citizenship? Certainly, there can be no guarantee that further political socialisation of member state nationals into the European integration process will be either easy or ultimately successful. However, if it is not attempted, this book demonstrates that EU democratisation is unlikely ever to develop beyond the extremely problematic, partial, Schumpeterian status it has currently attained.

Democracy is an inherently idealistic concept, albeit one which is intrinsic to the good functioning of society, and so I make no excuse for ending a book which has attempted to bring theoretical enquiry and empirical investigation together in an explicitly normative fashion. As Zürn remarks:

> Ultimately, democratic governance beyond the nation-state is based on a political and moral vision of reflective self-regulation by self-governing individuals and organisations who are prepared to forgo their own rational interests if there are good universalistic reasons for public-interested oriented behaviour. (2000: 212)

Europeans deserve a more democratic EU than they currently have, but the responsibility for securing it is not solely on the shoulders of elites at national or European level. Individuals too have a moral duty to demand and exploit a process of political socialisation into the EU system, in order to fulfil both utilitarian calculations (obtaining what they can from EU policy) and their responsibilities as citizens of a complex, highly interdependent transnational political system whose essence will not be transformed without their intervention, facilitated by suitable structures. Critical deliberativism ultimately rests on individuals using the opportunities they have to take control of their lives with suitable regard to the needs and preferences of others. Aux armes, citoyens!

NOTE

1   Those interested in detailed reform proposals from a different but complementary perspective might also wish to consult Philippe Schmitter's masterly contribution to the debate (Schmitter 2000). Intriguing visions of the EU's future institutional order can be found in Grant (2000) and Bertrand et al. (1999).

Bibliography

Abromeit, H. (1998) 'How to Democratise a Multi-level, Multi-dimensional Polity' in A. Weale and M. Nentwich (eds) *Political Theory and the European Union*. London: Routledge.

Adonnino Committee (Ad hoc Committee on a People's Europe) (1985) *A People's Europe – Reports from the Ad Hoc Committee* (Bulletin of the European Communities, Supplement 7/85) Luxembourg: Office for Official Publications of the European Communities CB-NF-85-007-EN-C.

Alexander, J. (1991) 'Habermas and Critical Theory: Beyond the Marxian Dilemma?', in A. Honneth and H. Joas (eds) *Communicative Action: Essays on Jürgen Habermas's 'The Theory of Communicative Action'*. Cambridge: Polity.

Allen, D. (2000) 'Cohesion and the Structural Funds', in H. Wallace and W. Wallace (eds) *Policy Making in the European Union* (4th edn). Oxford: Oxford University Press.

Almond, G. and Verba, S. (1963) *The Civic Culture*. Princeton, NJ: Princeton University Press.

Alter, K. and Meunier-Aitsahalia, S. (1994) 'Judicial Politics in the European Community: European Integration and the Pathbreaking *Cassis-de-Dijon* Decision', *Comparative Political Studies* 26:4, 535–61.

Andersen, S. and Burns, T. (1996) 'The European Union and the Erosion of Parliamentary Democracy: A Study of Post-parliamentary Governance' in S. Andersen and K. Eliassen (eds) *The European Union: How Democratic Is It?* London: Sage.

Andersen, S. and Eliassen, K. (1996) 'Introduction: Dilemmas, Contradictions and the Future of European Democracy', in S. Andersen and K. Eliassen (eds) *The European Union: How Democratic Is It?* London: Sage.

Arblaster, A. (1987) *Democracy*. Milton Keynes: Open University Press.

Armand, L. and Drancourt, M. (1970) *The European Challenge*. London: Weidenfeld and Nicolson.

Bache, I. (1998) *The Politics of European Union Regional Policy: Multi-level Governance or Flexible Gatekeeping?* Sheffield: Sheffield Academic Press.

Bache, I. (1999) 'The Extended Gatekeeper: Central Government and the Implementation of EC Regional Policy in the UK', *Journal of European Public Policy* 6:1, 28–45.

Bache, I. and Jones, R. (2000) 'Has EU Regional Policy Empowered the Regions? A Study of Spain and the United Kingdom', *Regional and Federal Studies* 10:3, 1–20.

Bailey, I. (1999) 'Flexibility, Harmonization and the Single Market in EU Environmental Policy: The Packaging Waste Directive', *Journal of Common Market Studies* 37:4, 549–71.

Balanyá, B., Doherty, A., Hoederman, O., Ma'anit, A. and Wesselius, E. (2000) *Europe Inc: Regional and Global Restructuring and the Rise of Corporate Power.* London: Pluto Press.

Banchoff, T. and Smith, M. (1999) 'Introduction: Conceptualizing Legitimacy in a Contested Polity', in T. Banchoff and M. Smith (eds) *Legitimacy and the European Union.* London: Routledge.

Bañkowski, Z. and Scott, A. (1996) 'The European Union?' in R. Bellamy (ed.) *Constitutionalism, Democracy and Sovereignty: American and European Perspectives.* Aldershot: Avebury.

Barnes, P. and Barnes, I. (1999) *Environmental Policy in the European Union.* Cheltenham: Edward Elgar.

Bauböck, R. (1994) *Transnational Citizenship: Membership and Rights in International Migration.* Aldershot: Edward Elgar.

Beetham, D. (1994) 'Key Principles and Indices for a Democratic Audit' in D. Beetham (ed.) *Defining and Measuring Democracy.* London: Sage.

Beetham, D. and Lord, C. (1998) 'Legitimacy and the European Union' in A. Weale and M. Nentwich (eds) *Political Theory and the European Union.* London: Routledge.

Behrens, P. and Smyrl, M. (1999) 'A Conflict of Rationalities: EU Regional Policy and the Single Market', *Journal of European Public Policy* 6:3, 419–35.

Bellamy, R. (1993) 'Liberalism', in R. Eatwell and A. Wright (eds) *Contemporary Political Ideologies.* London: Pinter.

Bellamy, R. (1995) 'The Constitution of Europe: Rights or Democracy?', in R. Bellamy, V. Buffacchi and D. Castiglione (eds) *Democracy and Constitutional Culture in the Union of Europe.* London: Lothian.

Bellamy, R. (1996) 'Introduction: Constitutionalism, Democracy and Sovereignty' in R. Bellamy (ed.) *Constitutionalism, Democracy and Sovereignty: American and European Perspectives.* Aldershot: Avebury.

Bellamy, R. (2001) 'The "Right to Have Rights": Citizenship Practice and the Political Constitution of the EU' in R. Bellamy and A. Warleigh (eds) *Citizenship and Governance in the European Union.* London: Continuum.

Bellamy, R. and Castiglione, D. (1996) 'The Communitarian Ghost in the Cosmopolitan Machine: Constitutionalism, Democracy and the Reconfiguration of Politics in the New Europe' in R. Bellamy (ed.) *Constitutionalism, Democracy and Sovereignty: American and European Perspectives.* Aldershot: Avebury.

Bellamy, R. and Castiglione, D. (1997) 'Building the Union: The Nature of Sovereignty in the Political Architecture of Europe', *Law and Philosophy* 16, 421–45.

Bellamy, R. and Castiglione, D. (1998) 'The Normative Challenge of a European Polity: Cosmopolitan and Communitarian Models Compared, Criticised and

Combined' in A. Follesdal and P. Koslowski (eds) *Democracy and the European Union*. Heidelberg: Springer.

Bellamy, R. and Castiglione, D. (2000a) *The Normative Turn in European Union Studies: Legitimacy, Identity and Democracy*. University of Exeter: RUSEL Working Paper 38.

Bellamy, R. and Castiglione, D. (2000b) 'Democracy, Sovereignty and the Constitution of the European Union: The Republican Alternative to Liberalism' in Z. Bañkowski and A. Scott (eds) *The European Union and Its Order: The Legal Theory of European Integration*. Oxford: Blackwell.

Bellamy, R. and Warleigh, A. (1998) 'From an Ethics of Integration to an Ethics of Participation: Citizenship and the Future of the European Union', *Millennium* 27:3, 447–68.

Bellamy, R. and Warleigh, A. (eds) (2001) *Citizenship and Governance in the European Union*. London: Continuum.

Bellamy, R. and Warleigh, A. (2001) 'Introduction: The Puzzle of European Citizenship', in R. Bellamy and A. Warleigh (eds) *Citizenship and Governance in the European Union*. London: Continuum.

Bertrand, G., Michalski, A. and Pench, L. (1999) *Scenarios Europe 2010: Five Possible Futures for Europe*. Brussels: Forward Studies Unit, European Commission.

Blondel, J., Sinnott, R. and Svensson, P. (1998) *People and Parliament in the European Union: Participation, Democracy and Legitimacy*. Oxford: Clarendon.

Bomberg, E. and Peterson, J. (1998) 'European Union Decision-Making: The Role of Sub-national Authorities', *Political Studies* 46:2, 219–35.

Bosco, A. (1996) 'What is Federalism? Towards a General Theory of Federalism: The Theory, The History and its Application to European Unification'. London: European Institute, South Bank University European Paper 1/96.

Bradley, K.St.C. (1987) 'Maintaining the Balance: The Role of the Court of Justice in Defining the Institutional Position of the European Parliament', *Common Market Law Review* 24, 41–64.

Bradley, K.St.C. (1991) 'Sense and Sensibility: Parliament v. Council Continued', *European Law Review* 16:3, 245–57.

Brown, C. (1992) *International Relations Theory: New Normative Approaches*. Hemel Hempstead: Harvester Wheatsheaf.

Bulmer, S. (1994) 'Institutions and Policy Change in the European Communities: The Case of Merger Control', *Public Administration* 72:3, 423–44.

Bulmer, S. (1996) 'the European Council and the Council of the European Union: Shapers of a European Confederation?', *Publius* 26:4, 17–42.

Bunyan, T. (1999) *Secrecy and Openness in the EU*. London: Kogan Page.

Burgess, M. (1989) *Federalism and European Union*. London: Routledge.

Burns, C. (2001) 'The European Parliament', in A. Warleigh (ed.) *Understanding European Union Institutions*. London: Routledge.

Camilleri, J. and Falk, J. (1992) *The End of Sovereignty? The Politics of a Shrinking and Fragmenting World*. Aldershot: Edward Elgar.

Caporaso, J. (1996) 'The European Union and Forms of State: Westphalian, Regulatory or Post-Modern?', *Journal of Common Market Studies* 34:1, 29–52.

CEC (Commission of the European Communities) (2001) *European Governance: A White Paper*. Brussels: European Commission COM (2001) 428.

Chaltiel, F. (1998) 'Le Traité d'Amsterdam et la Coopération Renforcée', *Revue du Marché Commun et de l'Union Européenne* 418: 289–93.

Chambers, S. (1996) *Reasonable Democracy: Jürgen Habermas and the Politics of Discourse*. Ithaca/London: Cornell University Press.

Christiano, T. (1997) 'The Significance of Public Deliberation' in J. Bohman and W. Rehg (eds) *Deliberative Democracy: Essays on Reason and Politics*. London/Cambridge, MA: MIT Press.

Christiansen, T., Jørgensen, K.E. and Wiener, A. (eds) (1999) *The Social Construction of Europe*. Special Issue of the *Journal of European Public Policy* 6:4.

Chryssochoou, D. (1998) *Democracy in the European Union*. London: Tauris.

Chryssochoou, D. (2000) 'Meta-Theory and the Study of the European Union: Capturing the Normative Turn', *Journal of European Integration* 22, 123–44.

Chryssochoou, D. (2001a) 'The Nature of Democracy in the European Union and the Limits of Treaty Reform', *Current Politics and Economics of Europe* 10:3, 245–64.

Chryssochoou, D. (2001b) *Theorizing European Integration*. London: Sage.

Chryssochoou, D., Stavridis, S. and Tsinisizelis, M. (1998) 'European Democracy, Parliamentary Decline and the "Democratic Deficit" of the European Union', *Journal of Legislative Studies*, 4:3, 108–28.

Closa, C. (1996) *A New Social Contract? EU Citizenship as the Institutional Basis of a New Social Contract: Some Sceptical Remarks* (RSC Paper 96/48). Florence: European University Institute.

Closa, C. (1998a) 'Some Foundations for the Normative Discussion on Supranational Citizenship and Democracy' in U. Preuss and F. Requejo (eds) *European Citizenship, Multiculturalism and the State*. Baden Baden: Nomos.

Closa, C. (1998b) 'Supranational Citizenship and Democracy: Normative and Empirical Dimensions', in M. Torre (eds) *European Citizenship: An Institutional Challenge*. Dordrecht: Kluwer.

Closa, C. (2001) 'Requirements of a European Public Sphere: Civil Society, Self, and the Institutionalization of Citizenship', in K. Eder and B. Giesen (eds) *European Citizenship Between National Legacies and Transnational Projects*. Oxford: Oxford University Press.

Cohen, J. (1997) 'Deliberation and Democratic Legitimacy', in J Bohman and W Rehg (eds) *Deliberative Democracy: Essays on Reason and Politics*. London/Cambridge, MA: MIT Press.

Collins, K. (1997) 'Integrating Sustainability: The Environmental Agenda of the European Parliament', Speech to COSLA, 24 January.

Collins, K., Burns, C. and Warleigh, A. (1998) 'Policy Entrepreneurs: The Role of European Parliament Committees in the Making of EU Policy', *Statute Law Review* 19:1, 1–11.

Collins, K. and Earnshaw, D. (1993) 'The Implementation and Enforcement of EC Environment Legislation', in D. Judge (ed.) *A Green Dimension for the European Community*. London: Cass.

Conzelmann, T. (1998) '"Europeanization" of Regional Development Policies? Linking the Multi-level Governance Approach with Theories of Policy Learning and Policy Change', European Integration on-line Papers 2:4, http://eiop.or.at/eiop/texte/1998-004a.htm

Corbett, R. (1989) 'Testing the New Procedures: The EP's First Experiences with Its New "Single Act" Powers', *Journal of Common Market Studies* 27:4, 359–72.

Corbett, R. (1998) *The European Parliament's Role in Closer European Integration*. London: Macmillan.

Cram, L. (2001) 'Imagining the Union: A Case of Banal Europeanism?' in H. Wallace (ed.) *Interlocking Dimensions of European Integration*. Basingstoke: Palgrave.

Crombez, C. (2001) 'The Treaty of Amsterdam and the Codecision Procedure' in G. Schneider and M. Aspinwall (eds) *The Rules of Integration: Institutionalist Approaches to the Study of Europe*. Manchester: Manchester University Press.

Curtin, D. (1997) *Postnational Democracy: The European Union in Search of a Political Philosophy*. The Hague: Kluwer.

Dahl, R. (1982) *Dilemmas of Pluralist Democracy: Autonomy vs. Control*. New Haven, CT/London: Yale University Press.

Dahl, R. (1989) *Democracy and Its Critics*. New Haven, CT; London: Yale University Press.

Dankert, P. (1997) 'Pressure from the European Parliament', in G Edwards and A. Pijpers (eds) *The Politics of European Treaty Reform*. London: Pinter.

Davidson, A. (1997) 'Regional Politics: the European Union and Citizenship', *Citizenship Studies* 1:1, 33–55.

Davies, N. (1997) *Europe: A History*. London: Pimlico.

Dawisha, K. (1990) *Eastern Europe, Gorbachev and Reform: The Great Challenge* (2nd edn) Cambridge: Cambridge University Press.

Day, S. and Shaw, J. (2000) 'Implementing Union Citizenship: The Case of Alien Suffrage and the European Union'. Paper to TSER Workshop *The Constitution of European Democracy*, Institute for Advanced Studies, Vienna 29/9/00–1/10/00.

De Búrca, G. (1998) 'The Principle of Subsidiarity and the Court of Justice as an Institutional Actor', *Journal of Common Market Studies* 36:2, 217–35.

De Rynck, S. and McAleavey, P. (2001) 'The Cohesion Deficit in Structural Fund Policy', *Journal of European Public Policy* 8:4, 541–57.

Dehousse, R. (1995) 'Constitutional Reform in the European Community: Are There Alternatives to the Majority Avenue?', *West European Politics* 18:3, 118–36.

Devuyst, Y. (1998) 'Treaty Reform in the European Union: The Amsterdam Process', *Journal of European Public Policy* 5:4, 615–31.

Devuyst, Y. (1999) 'The Community Method After Amsterdam', *Journal of Common Market Studies* 37:1, 109–20.

Dinan, D. (1997) 'The Commission and the Reform Process', in G. Edwards and A. Pijpers (eds) *The Politics of European Treaty Reform*. London: Pinter.

Dinan, D. (1999) *Ever Closer Union: An Introduction to European Integration* (2nd edn). Basingstoke: Macmillan.

Downes, T. (2001) 'Market Citizenship: Functionalism and Fig-leaves' in R. Bellamy and A. Warleigh (eds) *Citizenship and Governance in the European Union*. London: Continuum.

Dryzek, J. (1990) *Discursive Democracy: Politics, Policy and Political Science*. Cambridge: Cambridge University Press.

Dryzek, J. (1996) *Democracy in Capitalist Times*. Oxford: Oxford University Press.

Dryzek, J. (2000) *Deliberative Democracy and Beyond: Liberals, Critics, Contestations*. Oxford: Oxford University Press.

Duchesne, S. and Frognier, A.-P. (1995) 'Is There a European Identity?', in O. Niedermayer and R. Sinnott (eds) *Public Opinion and Internationalized Governance*. Oxford: Oxford University Press.

Duff, A. (1997) *The Treaty of Amsterdam: Text and Commentary*. London: Federal Trust/Sweet and Maxwell.

Duff, A., Pinder, J. and Pryce, F. (eds) (1994) *Maastricht and Beyond: Building the European Union*. London: Routledge.

Dyson, K. (1980) *The State Tradition in Western Europe*. Oxford: Martin Roberston.

Earnshaw, D. and Judge, D. (1995) *Prelude to Codecision: A Qualitative Assessment of the Cooperation Procedure in the 1989–94 European Parliament*. Luxembourg: European Parliament Directorate General for Research Project IV/93/54.

Earnshaw, D. and Judge, D. (1996) 'From Cooperation to Codecision: The European Parliament's Path to Legislative Power' in J. Richardson (ed.) *European Union: Power and Policy Making*. London: Routledge.

Ehlermann, C.-D. (1988) 'Differentiation, Flexibility, Closer Cooperation: The New Provisions of the Amsterdam Treaty', *European Law Journal* 4:3, 246–70.

Elster, J. (1997) 'The Market and the Forum: Three Varieties of Political Theory', in J. Bohman and W. Rehg (eds) *Deliberative Democracy: Essays on Reason and Politics*. London/Cambridge, MA: MIT Press.

Emiliou, N. (1992) 'Subsidiarity: An Effective Barrier Against the "Enterprises of Ambition"'?, *European Law Review* 17, 383–407.

Eriksen, E.O. (2000) 'Deliberative Supranationalism in the EU' in E.O. Eriksen and J.E. Fossum (eds) *Democracy in the European Union: Integration Through Deliberation?* London: Routledge.

Everson, M. and Preuss, U. (1995) *Concepts, Foundations and Limits of European Citizenship*. Bremen: Zentrum für Europäische Rechtspolitik.

Everts, P. and Sinnott, R. (1995) 'Conclusion: European Publics and the Legitimacy of Internationalised Governance' in O. Niedermayer and R. Sinnott (eds) *Public Opinion and Internationalized Governance*. Oxford: Oxford University Press.

Fairbrass, J. and Jordan, A. (2001) 'Protecting Biodiversity in the European Union: National Barriers and European Opportunities?', *Journal of European Public Policy* 8:4, 499–518.

Featherstone, K. (1994) 'Jean Monnet and the "Democratic Deficit" in the European Union', *Journal of Common Market Studies* 32:2, 149–70.

Ferrajoli, L. (1996) 'Beyond Sovereignty and Citizenship: Towards a Global Constitutionalism' in R. Bellamy (ed.) *Constitutionalism, Democracy and Sovereignty: American and European Perspectives*. Aldershot: Avebury.

Follesdal, A. (2000) 'Subsidiarity and Democratic Deliberation' in E.O. Eriksen and J.E. Fossum (eds) *Democracy in the European Union: Integration through Deliberation?* London: Routledge.

Follesdal, A. and Koslowski, P. (eds) (1998) *Democracy and the European Union*. Heidelberg: Springer.

Forsyth, M. (1981) *Unions of States: The Theory and Practice of Confederation*. Leicester: Leicester University Press.

Fukuyama, F. (1992) *The End of History and the Last Man*. London: Hamish Hamiliton.

Gabel, M. (1998a) 'The Endurance of Supranational Governance: A Consociational Interpretation of the European Union', *Comparative Politics* 30:4, 463–75.

Gabel, M. (1998b) *Interests and Integration: Market Liberalisation, Public Opinion and European Union*. Ann Arbor: University of Michigan Press.

Garman, J. and Hilditch, L. (1998) 'Behind the Scenes: An Examination of the Informal Processes at Work in Conciliation', *Journal of European Public Policy* 5:2, 271–84.

Garrett, G. and Tsebelis, G. (1996) 'An Institutional Critique of Intergovern-mentalism', *International Organisation* 50:2, 269–99.

Gaus, G. (1997) 'Reason, Justification and Consensus: Why Democracy Can't Have It All', in J. Bohman and W. Rehg (eds) *Deliberative Democracy: Essays on Reason and Politics*. London/Cambridge, MA: MIT Press.

George, S. (1994) *An Awkward Partner: Britain in the European Community* (2nd edn). Oxford: Oxford University Press.

Geuss, R. (1981) *The Idea of a Critical Theory: Habermas and the Frankfurt School*. Cambridge: Cambridge University Press.

Gillespie, P. (1997) 'The Promise and Practice of Flexibility', in B. Tonra (ed.) *Amsterdam: What the Treaty Means*. Dublin: Institute of European Affairs.

Gillespie, P. (2001) 'Enhanced Cooperation', in J. Dooge and P. Keatinge (eds) *What The Treaty of Nice Means*. Dublin: Institute for European Affairs.

Grant, C. (2000) *EU 2010: An Optimistic Vision of the Future*. London: Centre for European Reform.

Green, P. (1994) 'Subsidiarity and European Union: Beyond the Ideological Impasse?', *Policy and Politics* 22:4, 287–300.

Greenwood, J. (1997) *Representing Interests in the European Union*. London: Macmillian.

Greenwood, J. and Ronit, K. (1994) 'Interest Groups in the European Community: Newly Emerging Dynamics and Forms', *West European Politics* 17:1, 31–52.

Gustavsson, S. (1998) 'Double Asymmetry as a Normative Challenge' in A. Follesdal and P. Koslowski (eds) *Democracy and the European Union*. Heidelberg: Springer.

Haas, E. (1964) *Beyond the Nation State: Functionalism and International Organization.* Stanford, CA: Stanford University Press.

Haas, E. (1968) *The Uniting of Europe: Political, Social and Economic Forces 1950–1957* (2nd edn). Stanford, CA: Stanford University Press.

Haas, E. (1975) *The Obsolescence of Regional Integration Theory.* Berkeley, CA: University of California Press.

Habermas, J. (1984) *Theory of Communicative Action, Volume I.* London: Heinemann.

Habermas, J. (1987) *Theory of Communicative Action, Volume II.* Cambridge: Polity.

Habermas, J. (1996) 'The European Nation State: Its Achievements and Its Limitations. On the Past and Future of Sovreeignty and Citizenship', *Ratio Juris* 9:2, 125–37.

Habermas, J. (2000) 'Beyond the Nation-State? On Some Consequences of Economic Globalization', in E.O. Eriksen and J.E. Fossum (eds) *Democracy in the European Union: Integration through Deliberation?* London: Routledge.

Hancock, J.R. (1941/4) *Plan for Action.* London: Whitcomb and Toombs.

Harrison, R.J. (1974) *Europe in Question.* London: Allen and Unwin.

Harste, G. (1998) 'The Democratic Surplus in the Construction of the EU', paper presented to the workshop on Social Constructivism and European Studies, Aarhus, 26–28 June.

Hedetoft, U. (1997) 'The Cultural Semiotics of "European Identity": Between National Sentiment and the Transnational Imperative', in A. Landau and R. Whitman (eds) *Rethinking the European Union.* London: Macmillan.

Held, D. (1988) *Models of Democracy.* Oxford: Polity.

Held, D. (1993) 'Democracy: From City-states to a Cosmopolitan Order?' in D. Held *Prospects for Democracy: North, South, East, West.* Cambridge: Polity.

Held, D. (1997) *Models of Democracy.* Cambridge: Polity.

Héritier, A. (1999) 'Elements of Democratic Legitimation in Europe: An Alternative Perspective', *Journal of European Public Policy* 6:2, 269–82.

Hix, S. (1999) *The Political System of the European Union.* London: Macmillan.

Hix, S. (2001) 'Legislative Behaviour and Party Competition in the European Parliament: An Application of NOMINATE to the EU', *Journal of Common Market Studies* 39:4, 663–88.

Hobsbawm, E. (1994) *Age of Extremes: The Short Twentieth Century 1914–1991.* London: Abacus.

Hobsbawm, E. (1997) *The Age of Capital 1848–1875.* London: Weidenfeld and Nicolson.

Hodges, M. (1978) 'Integration Theory', in T. Taylor (ed.) *Approaches and Theory in International Relations.* London: Longman.

Höffe, O. (1996) 'Subsidiarity as a Principle in the Philosophy of Government', *Regional and Federal Studies* 6:3, 56–73.

Holland, M. (1994) *European Integration: From Community to Union.* London: Pinter.

Hooghe, L. (1996a) 'Building a Europe with the Regions: The Changing Role of the European Commission', in L. Hooghe (ed.) *Cohesion Policy and European Integration: Building Multi-level Governance*. Oxford: Clarendon.

Hooghe, L. (1996b) 'Introduction: Reconciling EU-Wide Policy with National Diversity', in L. Hooghe (ed.) *Cohesion Policy and European Integration: Building Multilevel Governance*. Oxford: Clarendon.

Hooghe, L. (1998) 'EU Cohesion Policy and Competing Models of European Capitalism', *Journal of Common Market Studies* 36:4, 457–77.

Hooghe, L. and Keating, M. (1994) 'The Politics of European Union Regional Policy', *Journal of European Public Policy* 1:3, 367–93.

Höreth, M. (1999) 'No Way Out for the Beast? The Unsolved Legitimacy Problem of European Governance', *Journal of European Public Policy* 6:2, 249–68.

Howe, P. (1995) 'A Community of Europeans: The Requisite Underpinnings', *Journal of Common Market Studies* 33:1, 27–46.

Hunt, J. (2001) 'The European Court of Justice and the Court of First Instance' in A. Warleigh (ed.) *Understanding European Union Institutions*. London: Routledge.

Jachtenfuchs, M., Diez, T. and Jung, S. (1998) 'Which Europe? Conflicting Models of a Legitimate European Order', *European Journal of International Relations* 4:4, 409–45.

Jeffery, C. (2000) 'Sub-national Mobilisation and European Integration: Does it Make Any Difference?', *Journal of Common Market Studies* 38:1, 1–23.

Joerges, C. (1996) 'Taking the Law Seriously: On Political Science and the Role of Law in the Process of European Integration', *European Law Journal* 2:2, 105–35.

Joerges, C. (1997) 'The Impact of European Integration on Private Law: Reductionist Perceptions, True Conflicts and a New Constitutional Perspective', *European Law Journal* 3:4, 378–406.

Judge, D. (1992) 'Predestined to Save the Earth? The Environment Committee of the European Parliament', *Environmental Politics* 1:4, 186–212.

Judge, D. (1993) 'Introduction: A Green Dimension for the European Community' in D. Judge (ed.) *A Green Dimension for the European Community*. London: Cass.

Judge, D. and Earnshaw, D. (1994) Weak European Parliament Influence? A Study of the Environment Committee of the European Parliament', *Government and Opposition* 29:2, 262–76.

Kaldor, M. and Vejvoda, I. (1999) 'Democratization in Central and East European Countries: An Overview' in M. Kaldor and I. Vejvoda (eds) *Democratization in Central and Eastern Europe*. London: Pinter.

Keating, M. and Hooghe, L. (2001) 'By-passing the Nation State? Regions and the EU Policy Process', in J. Richardson (ed.) *European Union: Power and Policy-Making* (2nd edn). London: Routledge.

Keck, M. and Sikkink, K. (1998) *Activists Beyond Borders: Advocacy Networks in International Politics*. Ithaca, NY: Cornell University Press.

Kellow, A. and Zito, A. (2002) 'Steering Through Complexity: EU Environmental Regulation in the International Context', *Political Studies* 50:1, 43–60.

Kelstrup, M. and Williams. M. (eds) (2000) *International Relations Theory and the Politics of European Integration: Power, Security and Community*. London: Routledge.

Keohane, R. and Hoffmann, S. (1991) 'Institutional Change in Europe in the 1980s' in R. Keohane and S. Hoffmann (eds) *The New European Community: Decision-making and Institutional Change*. Boulder, CO: Westview Press.

King, P. (1982) *Federalism and Federation*. London: Croon Helm.

Klein, N. (2000) *No Logo*. London: Flamingo.

Knill, C. (2001) *The Europeanisation of National Administrations: Patterns of Institutional Change and Persistence*. Cambridge: Cambridge University Press.

Kohler-Koch, B. (2000) 'Framing: The Bottleneck of Constructing Legitimate Institutions', *Journal of European Public Policy* 7:4, 513–31.

Kortenberg, H. (2000) 'Closer Cooperation in the Treaty of Amsterdam', *Common Market Law Review* 35: 833–54.

Koslowski, P. (1998) 'Fatherland Europe? On European and National Identity and Democratic Sovereignty' in A. Follesdal and P. Koslowski (eds) *Democracy and the European Union*. Heidelberg: Springer.

Kostakopoulou, T. (2001) *Citizenship, Identity and Immigration in the European Union*. Manchester: Manchester University Press.

Krasner, S. (1999) *Sovereignty: Organized Hypocrisy*. Princeton, NJ: Princeton University Press.

Kraus, P. (2000) 'Political Unity and Linguistic Diversity in Europe', *European Sociology Journal* XLI.1, 138–63.

Laffan, B. (1996) 'The Politics of Identity and Political Order in Europe', *Journal of Common Market Studies* 34:1, 81–102.

Laffan, B. (1998) 'The European Union: A Distinctive Model of Internationalization', *Journal of European Public Policy* 5:2, 235–53.

Laffan, B., O'Donnell, R. and Smith, M. (2000) *Europe's Experimental Union: Rethinking Integration*. London: Routledge.

Lambert, J. and Hoskyns, C. (2000) 'How Democratic is the European Parliament?' in C. Hoskyns and M. Newman (eds) *Democratizing the European Union: Issues for the Twenty-First Century*. Manchester: Manchester University Press.

Lamers, K. (1997) 'Strengthening the Hard Core', in P. Gowan and P. Anderson (eds) *The Question of Europe*. London: Verso.

Laqueur, W. (1982) *Europe Since Hitler: The Rebirth of Europe*. London: Penguin.

Lévêque, F. (1996a) 'The European Fabric of Environmental Regulations' in F. Lévêque (ed.) *Environmental Policy in Europe*. Cheltenham: Edward Elgar.

Lévêque, F. (1996b) 'Introduction' in F. Lévêque (ed.) *Environmental Policy in Europe*. Cheltenham: Edward Elgar.

Lévêque, F. (1996c) 'Conclusion' in F. Lévêque (ed.) *Environmental Policy in Europe*. Cheltenham: Edward Elgar.

Levine, A. (1981) *Liberal Democracy: A Critique of its Theory*. New York: Columbia University Press.

Lewis, J. (2000) 'The Methods of Community in EU Decision Making and Administrative Rivalry in the Council's Infrastructure', *Journal of European Public Policy* 7:2, 261–89.

Lindberg, L. and Scheingold, S. (1970) *Europe's Would-Be Polity*. Englewood Cliffs, NJ: Prentice-Hall.

Lindberg, L. and Scheingold, S. (1971) *Regional Integration: Theory and Research*. Cambridge, NH: Harvard University Press.

Linklater, A. (1998) *The Transformation of Political Community: Ethical Foundations of the Post-Westphalian Era*. Cambridge: Polity.

Lodge, J. (1994) 'Transparency and Democratic Legitimacy', *Journal of Common Market Studies* 32:3, 343–68.

Lodge, J. and Herman, V. (1982) *Direct Elections to the European Parliament*. London: Macmillan.

Lord, C. (1998a) *Democracy in the European Union*. Sheffield: Sheffield Academic Press.

Lord, C. (1998b) 'Introduction' in D. Bell and C. Lord (eds) *Transnational Parties in the European Union*. Aldershot: Ashgate.

Lord, C. (2001) 'Assessing Democracy in a Contested Polity', *Journal of Common Market Studies* 39:4, 641–61.

Lord, C. and Beetham, D. (2001) 'Legitimizing the European Union: Is there a "Post-Parliamentary Basis" for its Legitimation?', *Journal of Common Market Studies* 39:3, 443–62.

Loughlin, J. (1997) 'Regional Policy in the European Union' in S. Stavridis, E. Mossialos, R. Morgan and H. Machin (eds) *New Challenges to the European Union: Policies and Policy-Making*. Aldershot: Dartmouth.

MacCormick, N. (1999) *Questioning Sovereignty: Law, State and Nation in the European Commonwealth*. Oxford: Oxford University Press.

Macpherson, C.B. (1977) *The Life and Times of Liberal Democracy*. Oxford: Oxford University Press.

Magnette, P. (1999) *La Citoyenneté Européenne: Droits, Politiques, Institutions*. Brussels: Editions de l'Université de Bruxelles.

Majone, G. (1996) *Regulating Europe*. London: Routledge.

March, J. and Olsen, J. (1995) *Democratic Governance*. New York: Free Press.

Marin, A. (1997) 'EC Environment Policy', in S. Stavridis, E. Mossialos, R. Morgan and H. Machin (eds) *New Challenges to the European Union: Policies and Policy-Making*. Aldershot: Dartmouth.

Marks, G. (1996) 'Exploring and Explaining Variation in EU Cohesion Policy' in L. Hooghe (ed.) *Cohesion Policy and European Integration: Building Multi-level Governance*. Oxford: Clarendon.

Maurer, A. (1999) *(Co-)Governing After Maastricht: The European Parliament's Institutional Performance 1994–98. Lessons for the Implementation of the Treaty of Amsterdam*. Luxembourg: European Parliament Directorate General for Research, POLI 104.EN.

Meehan, E. (1993) *Citizenship and the European Community*. London: Sage.

Meehan, E. (2001) 'EU Citizenship and Pan-Europeanism', in H. Wallace (ed.) *Interlocking Dimensions of European Integration*. Basingstoke: Palgrave.

Mény, Y. and Knapp, A. (1998) *Government and Politics in Western Europe* (3rd edn). Oxford: Oxford University Press.

Miller, D. (1995) *On Nationality*. Oxford: Oxford University Press.

Milward, A. (1994) *The European Rescue of the Nation-State*. London: Routledge.

Mitrany, D. (1933) *The Progress of International Government*. London: Allen and Unwin.

Mitrany, D. (1944) *A Working Peace System*. London: Royal Institute of International Affairs.

Mitrany, D. (1965) 'The Prospect of Integration: Federal or Functional?', *Journal of Common Market Studies* 4:2, 119–49.

Mitrany, D. (1971) 'The Functional Approach in Historical Perspective', *International Affairs* 47:3, 532–43.

Mitrany, D. (1975) *The Functional Theory of Politics*. London: Martin Robertson.

Modood, T. (1997) 'Introduction: The Politics of Multiculturalism in the New Europe' in T. Modood and P. Werbner (eds) *The Politics of Multiculturalism in the New Europe: Racism, Identity and Community*. London: Zed.

Monnet, J. (1978) *Memoirs*. London: Collins.

Montani, G. (1993) 'European Citizenship and European Identity', *Federalist* Year 2, 95–125.

Moravcsik, A. (1991) 'Negotiating the Single European Act: National Interests and Conventional Statecraft in the European Community', *International Organization* 45:1, 19–56.

Moravcsik, A. (1993) 'Preferences and Power in the European Community: A Liberal Intergovernmentalist Approach', *Journal of Common Market Studies* 31:4, 473–524.

Moravcsik, A. (1999) *The Choice for Europe: Social Purpose and State Power from Messina to Maastricht*. London: UCL Press.

Moravcsik, A. and Nicolaidis, K. (1999) 'Explaining the Treaty of Amsterdam: Interests, Influence, Institutions', *Journal of Common Market Studies* 37:1, 59–85.

Murray, P. (1996) 'Spinelli and European Union' in P. Murray and P. Rich (eds) *Visions of European Unity*. Boulder, CO/Oxford: Westview.

Navari, C. (1996) 'Functionalism Versus Federalism: Alternative Visions of European Unity' in P. Murray and P. Rich (eds) *Visions of European Unity*. Boulder, CO/Oxford: Westview.

Nentwich, M. (1998) 'Opportunity Structures for Citizens' Participation: The Case of the European Union' in A. Weale and M. Nentwich (eds) *Political Theory and the European Union*. London: Routledge.

Neunreither, K. (1998) 'Governance Without Opposition: The Case of the European Union', *Government and Opposition* 33:4, 419–441.

Neunreither, K. (2000a) 'Political Representation in the European Union: A Common Whole, Various Wholes or Just a Hole?', in K. Neunreither and

A. Wiener (eds) *European Integration After Amsterdam: Institutional Dynamics and Prospects for Democracy*. Oxford: Oxford University Press.

Neunreither, K. (2000b) 'The European Union in Nice: A Minimalist Approach to a Historic Challenge', *Government and Opposition* 36:2, 184–208.

Newman, M. (1996) *Democracy, Sovereignty and the European Union*. London: Hurst.

Obradovic, D. (1996) 'Policy Legitimacy and the European Union', *Journal of Common Market Studies* 34:2, 191–221.

O'Leary, S. (1996) *European Union Citizenship: Options for Reform*. London: IPPR.

O'Neill. M. (2000) 'Theorising the European Union: Towards a Post-foundational Discourse', *Current Politics and Economics of Europe* 9:2, 121–45.

Pentland, C. (1973) *International Theory and European Integration*. London: Faber and Faber.

Pentland, C. (1975) 'Functionalism and Theories of International Political Integration', in A.J.R. Groom and P. Taylor (eds) *Functionalism: Theory and Practice in International Integration*. London: University of London Press.

Peterson, J. (1994) 'Subsidiarity: A Definition to Suit Any Vision?', *Parliamentary Affairs* 47:1, 116–32.

Philippart, E. (2001) 'The New Provisions on "Closer Cooperation": A Call for Prudent Politics', *European Community Studies Association Review* 14:2, 6–7.

Philippart, E. and Edwards, G. (1999) 'The Provisions on Closer Cooperation in the Treaty of Amsterdam: The Politics of Flexibility in the European Union', *Journal of Common Market Studies* 37:1, 87–108.

Pierson, P. (1996) 'The Path to European Integration: A Historical Institutionalist Analysis', *Comparative Political Studies* 29:2, 123–63.

Pinder, J. (1991) *European Community: The Building of a Union*. Oxford: Oxford University Press.

Pollack, M. (1995) 'Regional Actors in an Intergovernmental Play: The Making and Implementation of EC Structural Policy' in C. Rhodes and S. Mazey (eds) *The State of the European Union, Volume 3*. Boulder, CO: Lynne Rienner.

Pollack, M. (1999) 'Delegation, Agency and Agenda Setting in the Treaty of Amsterdam', *European Integration On-line Papers* 3:6, http://eiop.or.at/eiop/texte/1999-006a.htm

Pryce, R. (1994) 'The Maastricht Treaty and the New Europe' in A. Duff, J. Pinder and R. Pryce (eds) *Maastricht and Beyond: Building the European Union*. London: Routledge.

Raunio, T. (1999) 'Always One Step Behind? National Legislatures and the European Union', *Government and Opposition* 34:2, 180–202.

Raunio, T. and Hix, S. (2001) 'Backbenchers Learn to Fight Back: European Integration and Parliamentary Government' in K.H. Goetz and S. Hix (eds) *Europeanised Politics? European Integration and National Political Systems*. London: Frank Cass.

Rawls, J. (1971) *A Theory of Justice*. Cambridge, MA: Harvard University Press.

Rawls, J. (1997) 'The Idea of Public Reason' in J. Bohman and W. Rehg (eds) *Deliberative Democracy: Essays on Reason and Politics*. London/Cambridge, MA: MIT Press.

Reising, U. (1998) 'Domestic and Supranational Political Opportunities: European Protest in Selected Countries 1980–1995' European Integration On-line Papers 2:5. http://eiop.or.at/eiop/texte/1998-005a.htm

Risse, T. (2000) '"Let's Argue!": Communicative Action in World Politics', *International Organization* 54:1, 1–39.

Rosamond, B. (2000a) *Theories of European Integration*. Basingstoke: Macmillan.

Rosamond, B. (2000b) 'Theorising the European Union Past, Present and Future: On Knowledge, Disciplines and "Thinking Thoroughly" About Integration Theory', *Current Politics and Economics of Europe* 9:2, 147–63.

Sabine, G. (1939) *A History of Political Theory*. London: Harrap.

Sandholtz, W. and Zysman, J. (1989) '1992: Recasting the European Bargain', *World Politics* 27:4, 95–128.

Saward, M. (1994) 'Democratic Theory and Indices of Democratization' in D. Beetham (ed.) *Defining and Measuring Democracy*. London: Sage.

Sbragia, A. (2000) 'Environmental Policy: Economic Constraints and External Pressures' in H. Wallace and W. Wallace (eds) *Policy-Making in the European Union* (4th edn). Oxford: Oxford University Press.

Scharpf, F. (1999) *Governing in Europe: Effective and Democratic?* Oxford: Oxford University Press.

Schlesinger, P. and Kevin, D. (2000) 'Can the European Union Become a Sphere of Publics?', in E.O. Eriksen and J.E. Fossum (eds) *Democracy in the European Union: Integration Through Deliberation?* London: Routledge.

Schmitt, H. (1962) *The Path to European Union: From the Marshall Plan to the Common Market*. Baton Rouge, LA: Louisiana State University Press.

Schmitter, P. (1996a) 'Examining the Present Euro-Polity with the Help of Past Theories' in G. Marks, F. Scharpf, P. Schmitter and W. Streeck *Governance in the European Union*. London: Sage.

Schmitter, P. (1996b) 'Imagining the Future of the Euro-Polity with the Help of New Concepts' in G. Marks, F. Scharpf, P. Schmitter and W. Streeck *Governance in the European Union*. London: Sage.

Schmitter, P. (1998) 'Is It Really Possible to Democratize the Euro-Polity?' in A. Follesdal and P. Koslowski (eds) *Democracy and the European Union*. Heidelberg: Springer.

Schmitter, P. (2000) *How to Democratize the European Union ... And Why Bother?* New York: Rowman and Littlefield.

Scott, A., Peterson, J. and Millar, D. (1994) 'Subsidiarity: A "Europe of the Regions" v. The British Constitution?', *Journal of Common Market Studies* 32:1, 47–67.

Scully, R. (1997) 'The European Parliament and the Codecision Procedure: A Reassessment', *Journal of Legislative Studies* 3:3, 139–68.

Shackleton, M. (2000) 'The Politics of Codecision', *Journal of Common Market Studies* 38:2, 325–42.

Shaw, J. (1996) *Law of the European Union*. Basingstoke: Macmillan.

Shaw, J. (1998) 'The Treaty of Amsterdam: Challenges of Flexibility and Legitimacy', *European Law Journal* 4:1, 63–86.

Shaw, J. (2001) 'The Treaty of Nice: Legal and Constitutional Implications', *European Public Law* 7:2, 195–215.

Sherrington, P. (2000) *The Council of Ministers: Political Authority in the European Union*. London: Pinter.

Shore, C. and Black, A. (1994) 'Citizens' Europe and the Construction of European Identity' in V. Goddard, J. Llobera and C. Shore (eds) *The Anthropology of Europe: Identity and Boundaries in Conflict*. Oxford: Berg.

Siedentop, L. (2000) *Democracy in Europe*. London: Allen Lane/Penguin.

Sinnott, R. (1994) *Integration Theory, Subsidiarity and the Internationalisation of Issues: The Implications for Legitimacy*. Badia Fiesolana, Florence: European University Institute Working Paper 94/13.

Sloat, A. (2002) 'Governance: Contested Perceptions of Civic Participation', *Scottish Affairs* 39 (Spring), 103–17.

Smith, M. (1997) 'Democratic Deficit or Deficit of Democracy? European Integration and Privileged Institutional Position in Domestic Politics' in Y. Shain and A. Klieman (eds) *Democracy: The Challenges Ahead*. Basingstoke: Macmillan.

Smith, J. (1999) *Europe's Elected Parliament*. Sheffield: Sheffield Academic Press.

Sonntag, N. and Featherstone, K. (1984) 'Looking Towards the 1984 European Elections: Problems of Political Integration', *Journal of Common Market Studies* 23:3, 270–82.

Spicer, M. (1992) *A Treaty Too Far: A New Policy for Europe*. London: Fourth Estate.

Steiner, J. (1998) *European Democracies* (4th edn). London: Longman.

Stubb, A. (1996) 'A Categorisation of Differentiated Integration', *Journal of Common Market Studies* 34:2, 283–95.

Stubb, A. (1997) 'The 1996 IGC and the Management of Flexible Integration', *Journal of European Public Policy* 6:4, 579–97.

Sutcliffe, J. (2000) 'The 1999 Reform of the Structural Fund Regulations: Multi-level Governance or Renationalization?', *Journal of European Public Policy* 7:2, 290–309.

Taylor, C. (1998) 'The Dynamics of Democratic Exclusion', *Journal of Democracy* 9:4.

Taylor, P. (1975) 'The Politics of the European Communities: The Confederal Phase', *World Politics* April, 336–60.

Taylor, P. (1978a) 'A Conceptual Typology of International Organisation', in P. Taylor and A.J.R. Groom (eds) *International Organisation: A Conceptual Approach*. London: Pinter.

Taylor, P. (1978b) 'Functionalism: The Theory of David Mitrany', in P. Taylor and A.J.R. Groom (eds) *International Organisation: A Conceptual Approach*. London: Pinter.

Taylor, P. (1983) *The Limits of European Integration*. Beckenham: Croom Helm.

Taylor, P. (1996) *The European Union in the 1990s*. Oxford: Oxford University Press.

Thielemann, E. (2000) 'Institutional Change and European Governance: An Analysis of "Partnership"', *Current Politics and Economics of Europe* 9:2, 181–97.

Thielmann, E. (2002) 'The Price of Europeanization: Why European Regional Policy Initiatives are a Mixed Blessing', *Regional and Federal Studies* 12:1, 43–65.

Thompson, M. (1997) 'Why Democracy Does Not Always Follow Economic Ripeness' in Y. Shain and A. Klieman (eds) *Democracy: The Challenges Ahead*. Basingstoke: Macmillan.

Tinedmans, L. (1976) 'European Union: Report to the European Council', *Bulletin of the European Communities* Supplement 1/76. Luxembourg. Office of Official Publications of the EU.

Tömmel, I. (1998) 'Transformation of Governance: The European Commission's Strategy for Creating a "Europe of the Regions"', *Regional and Federal Studies* 8:2, 52–80.

Tranholm-Mikkelsen, J. (1991) 'Neofunctionalism: Obstinate or Obsolete? A Reappraisal in the Light of the New Dynamism of the EC', *Millennium* 20:1, 1–22.

Tsebelis, G. and Garrett, G. (2001) 'The Institutional Foundations of Inter-governmentalism and Supranationalism in the European Union', *International Organisation* 55:2, 357–90.

Tsebelis, G., Jensen, C., Kalandrakis, A. and Kreppel, A. (2001) 'Legislative Procedures in the European Union: An Empirical Analysis', *British Journal of Political Science* 31, 573–99.

Tuytschaever, F. (1999) *Differentiation in European Union Law*. Oxford: Hart.

Urwin, D. (1992) *The Community of Europe: A History of European Integration Since 1945*. London: Longman.

Van der Straaten, J. (1993) 'A Sound European Environmental Policy: Challenges, Possibilities and Barriers' in D. Judge (ed.) *A Green Dimension for the European Community*. London: Cass.

Van Hamme, A. (1988) 'The European Parliament and the Codecision Procedure', *Studia Diplomatica* 61:3, 291–314.

Van Parijs, P. (1998) 'Should the European Union Become More Democratic?' in A. Follesdal and P. Koslowski (eds) *Democracy and the European Union*. Heidelberg: Springer.

Vignon, J. (1993) 'Le Principe de Subsitiarité: Son Rôle et Sa Définition dans la Construction Européenne' in J. Monar, W. Ungerer and W. Wessels (eds) *The Maastricht Treaty on European Union: Legal Complexity and Political Dynamic*. Brussels: European Interuniversity Press.

Wallace, H. (2000) 'The Institutional Setting: Five Variations on a Theme', in H. Wallace and W. Wallace (eds) *Policy Making in the European Union* (4th edn). Oxford: Oxford University Press.

Wallace, W. (1990) *The Dynamics of European Integration*. London: Pinter/RIIA.

Wallace, W. (1997) 'The Nation-State: Rescue or Retreat?', in P. Gowan and P. Anderson (eds) *The Question of Europe*. London: Verso.

Walzer, M. (1983) *Spheres of Justice: A Defence of Pluralism and Equality*. Oxford: Martin Robertson.

Walzer, M. (1994) *Thick and Thin: Moral Argument at Home and Abroad*. Notre Dame, IN: University of Notre Dame Press.

Ward, I. (1997) 'Identity and Difference: The EU and Postmodernism', in J. Shaw and G. More (eds) *New Legal Dynamics of European Union*. Oxford: Clarendon.

Warleigh, A. (1998) 'Better the Devil You Know? Synthetic and Confederal Understandings of European Unification', *West European Politics* 21:3, 1–18.

Warleigh, A. (1999) *The Committee of the Regions: Institutionalising Multi-level Governance?* London: Kogan Page.

Warleigh, A. (2000a) 'The Hustle: Citizenship Practice, NGOs and "Policy Coalitions" in the European Union – The Cases of Auto Oil, Drinking Water and Unit Pricing', *Journal of European Public Policy* 7:2, 229–43.

Warleigh, A. (2000b) 'History Repeating? Framework Theory and Europe's Multi-level Confederation', *Journal of European Integration* 22, 173–200.

Warleigh, A. (2001a) 'Introduction: Institutions, Institutionalism and Decision-making in the European Union' in A. Warleigh (ed.) *Understanding European Union Institutions*. London: Routledge.

Warleigh, A. (2001b) 'Purposeful Opportunists? EU Institutions and the Struggle over European Citizenship' in R. Bellamy and A. Warleigh (eds) *Citizenship and Governance in the European Union*. London: Continuum.

Warleigh, A. (2001c) 'Europeanising Civil Society: NGOs as Agents of Political Socialization', *Journal of Common Market Studies* 39:4, 619–39.

Warleigh, A. (ed.) (2001d) *Understanding European Union Institutions*. London: Routledge.

Warleigh, A. (2001e) 'The Committee of the Regions' in A. Warleigh (ed.) *Understanding European Union Institutions*. London: Routledge.

Warleigh, A. (2002a) *Flexible Integration: Which Model for the European Union?* London: Continuum.

Warleigh, A. (2002b) 'Towards Network Democracy? The Potential of Flexible Integration' in M. Farrell, S. Fella and M. Newman (eds) *European Integration in the Twenty-First Century: Unity in Diversity?* London: Sage.

Warleigh, A. (2003) 'The European Union', in P. Burnell (ed.) *Democratisation Through the Looking-Glass*. Manchester: Manchester University Press.

Weale, A. (1997) 'Majority Rule, Political Identity and European Union', in P. Lehning and A. Weale (eds) *Citizenship, Democracy and Justice in the New Europe*. London: Routledge.

Weale, A. and Williams, A. (1993) 'Between Economy and Ecology? The Single Market and the Integration of Environmental Policy' in D. Judge (ed.) *A Green Dimension for the European Community*. London: Cass.

Webster, R. (1998) 'Environmental Collective Action: Stable Patterns of Co-operation and Issue Alliances at the European Level' in J. Greenwood and M. Aspinwall (eds) *Collective Action in the European Union: Interests and the New Politics of Associability*. London: Routledge.

Weigall, D. and Stirk, P. (1992) *The Origins and Development of the European Community*. Leicester: Leicester University Press.

Weiler, J.H.H. (1989) 'Pride and Prejudice: Parliament v. Council', *European Law Review* 14:5, 334–46.

Weiler, J.H.H. (1991) 'The Transformation of Europe', *Yale Law Review* 100, 2403–83.

Weiler, J.H.H. (1995) 'Does Europe Need a Constitution? Demos, Telos and the German Maastricht Decision', *European Law Journal* 1:3, 219–58.

Weiler, J.H.H., Haltern, U. and Mayer, F. (1995) 'European Democracy and its Critique', *West European Politics* 18:3, 4–39.

Wendt, A. (1987) 'The Agent-Structure Problem in International Relations Theory', *International Organization* 41:3, 335–70.

Wendt, A. (1999) *Social Theory of International Politics*. Cambridge: Cambridge University Press.

Wessels, W. (1997) 'An Ever Closer Fusion? A Dynamic Macropolitical View on Integration Processes', *Journal of Common Market Studies* 35:2, 267–99.

Westlake, M. (1994) *A Modern Guide to the European Parliament*. London: Routledge.

Wiener, A. (1996) 'Rethinking Citizenship: The Quest for Place-Oriented Participation in the EU', *Oxford International Review* Vol. 7, 44–51.

Wiener, A. (1998) *'European' Citizenship Practice: Building Institutions of a Non-state*. Boulder, CO: Westview Press.

Wiener, A. and Della Salla, V. (1997) 'Constitution-Making and Citizenship Practice: Bridging the Democracy Gap in the EU?', *Journal of Common Market Studies* 35:4, 595–614.

Williams, H., Wright, M. and Evans, T. (1993) *A Reader in International Relations and Political Theory*. Buckingham: Open University Press.

Wincott, D. (1995a) 'Institutional Interaction and European Integration: Towards an Everyday Critique of Liberal Intergovernmentalism', *Journal of Common Market Studies* 33:4, 597–609.

Wincott, D. (1995b) 'The Role of Law or the Rule of the Court of Justice? An "Institutional" Account of Judicial Politics in the European Community', *Journal of European Public Policy* 2:4, 583–602.

Wintrop, N. (1983) *Liberal Democratic Theory and Its Critics*. London: Croon Helm.

Young, H. (1998) *This Blessed Plot: Britain and Europe From Churchill to Blair*. Basingstoke: Macmillan.

Young, I.M. (1997) 'Difference as a Resource for Democratic Communication', in J. Bohman and W. Rehg (eds) *Deliberative Democracy: Essays on Reason and Politics*. London/Cambridge, MA: MIT Press.

Zellentin, G. (1962) 'The Economic and Social Committee', *Journal of Common Market Studies* 1:1, 22–28.

Zito, A. (2000) *Creating Environmental Policy in the European Union*. London: Macmillan.

Zürn, M. (2000) 'Democratic Governance Beyond the Nation-State: The EU and Other International Institutions', *European Journal of International Relations* 6:2, 183–221.

Index